Greavsies

SPORTS

QUIZ

CHALLENGE

Norman Giller

HAMLYN

To Irene and Eileenalana
They know all the answers

Acknowledgements

Quiz compiler Norman Giller wishes to thank Peter Arnold for his diligent editing, Piers Murray Hill for his motivating powers, Michael Giller for his Apple-a-day computer talent, artist David Edwards for his graphic support, *The Sun* for allowing me to use their daily teaser, The Name Game, and — most of all — James Greaves for letting me keep him puzzled for hours on end. Greavsie's scored yet again!

Published by The Hamlyn Publishing Group Limited
Bridge House, 69 London Road
Twickenham, Middlesex TW1 3SB, England
and distributed for them by
Octopus Distribution Services Limited
Rushden, Northamptonshire, England

Front cover photograph reproduced courtesy of TV-am.

First published in 1987

ISBN 0 600 55673 5
Printed in the United Kingdom

Contents

A Funny Old Game
By Jimmy Greaves

This is a sports book with a difference. You don't read it as much as *play* it. There's a challenge on every page and the ultimate test is to see if you can beat MY score. All the questions and puzzles have been compiled by quiz freak Norman Giller, author of more than 30 sports books and devisor of that argument-provoking ITV series, *Who's the Greatest?*   He is also the creator and compiler of *The Sun's* longest-running feature, *The Name Game,* and has at various times had more than 20 quiz and puzzle-game features published in national newspapers. In fact he's an all-round clever dick and one of the great bores of our time. His old mate Eric Morecambe once introduced him as, "This is Norman Giller, a man I've known and avoided for many years." That summed him up perfectly.

I've been trying to avoid him since we first got to know each other when we were both serving our apprenticeships — me learning how to get the ball across goal-lines at Chelsea, him learning how to catch deadlines on the *Stratford Express.* He then started haunting me as a sportswriter on the *Daily Herald* and the *Daily Express,* and since tunnelling his way out of Fleet Street to become a freeloader, sorry — freelance — 14 years ago he has nagged me into partnering him on ten book-writing ventures. Now comes this monster sports quiz book in which he insisted I become involved as a target setter. I took the Sports Challenge and my final score is recorded at the back of the book on page 190, along with a Ratings Guide so that you can judge whether you are a sports mastermind or, like me, somebody with just a better than average all-round knowledge of sport. I have exposed what I know about sport on national television as a resident captain on Central Television's enormously popular *Sporting Triangles* and I found 'Know-All' Norman's questions a good grounding for the weekly television examination.

The beauty of this book is that there is a challenge on every page. Your first target will be to beat the average score, then my score. Both my marks and the average score — assessed by testing an across-the-board mix of 100 sports fans of all ages — are printed in the introduction to each quiz. You can keep a check on your score and your running total in the scorecheck boxes at the bottom of each page. The answers to each quiz are at the foot of the next page but one, so you don't have to go searching around at the back of the book every few minutes to find out whether or not you are right. The first thing you'll need is a thick pad of paper and a pencil with plenty of lead in it so that you can make notes and jot down answers as you go along.

I managed to learn a few things from the quizzes that I did not know before accepting the Sports Challenge. For instance, I now know who was the father of identical twins who scored goals at identical times in each half of an FA Cup Final; and I can now name the former world heavyweight champion who once got involved in a bar-room brawl in a South Wales pub. But most of all, I learned that I must be out next time 'Know-All' Norman calls round with an idea. The man's a pain.

I'll get out of your way now and let you take up the Sports Challenge. I promise you, it's a funny old game!

1
WHO DID WHAT?

We kick off with a warm-up test. There are 10 points at stake, one point for each correct answer. Each answer is a surname that starts with the same initial.
Average score: 6 Greavsie: 8

1. WHO was the first British footballer sold for £1million?

2. WHO won a boxing gold medal for Britain in the middle-weight division in the 1968 Olympics in Mexico?

3. WHO is the former England cricket captain who is known to his team-mates as Gnome?

4. WHO was the Brazilian who won the world motor racing championship in 1972 and regained it in 1974?

5. WHO was the Australian who defeated Rod Laver in the 1960 men's singles final at Wimbledon?

6. WHO inspired a new style of 'flop' high jumping when he won an Olympic gold medal?

7. WHO was the first man to defeat Muhammad Ali?

8. WHO rode Red Rum to his first two victories in the Grand National at Aintree?

9. WHO was the footballing Preston plumber who was capped in four different forward positions for England?

10. WHO was known as the 'Pied Piper' of Gateshead?

ANSWERS

The answers to each quiz will appear on the next page but one. Keep a check on your score as you go along and then compare your final total with the RATINGS GUIDE on pages 190-191.

Your Score

Running Total

2 ODD MAN OUT

Who is the odd man out in each of the following six lists? We give you a little 'think hint' to help. Award yourself one point for each correct answer.
Average score: 3 Greavsie: 4

1. British heavyweight boxers Johnny Williams, Brian London, Joe Erskine, Henry Cooper, Dick Richardson, Joe Bugner, Jack Bodell. *Think titles.*

2. Manchester United footballers George Best, Bobby Charlton, Denis Law, David Sadler, John Aston, Brian Kidd, Pat Crerand. *Think European Cup.*

3. Olympic athletes Chris Brasher, Roger Bannister, Allan Wells, Douglas Lowe, Harold Abrahams, Eric Liddell, David Hemery. *Think medals.*

4. Test cricketers Len Hutton, Denis Compton, Peter May, Tony Greig, Mike Brearley, Ian Botham, Mike Gatting. *Think captains.*

5. Flat racing jockeys Gordon Richards, Scobie Breasley, Lester Piggott, Joe Mercer, Greville Starkey, Pat Eddery, Willie Carson. *Think Derbies.*

6. Welsh Rugby heroes Cliff Morgan, David Watkins, Gareth Edwards, Barry John, Phil Bennett, Malcolm Dacey, Jonathan Davies. *Think in halves!*

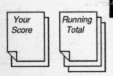

Your Score

Running Total

ANSWERS

You will find the answers to this Odd Man Out quiz on page 12.

3
SPORTSWORD

Award yourself one point for each clue that you solve correctly plus a bonus of 10 points if you complete the crossword.
Average score: 14
Greavsie: 24

ACROSS

1 He saved for England (5).
4 Walcott's name before he came to the top (5).
10 Town Hatters (5).
11 They are never alone at Ibrox (7).
12 Ian taking his time near goal? (2,2,4).
13 Zoff, who was always a handyman for Italy (4).
15 Boxers and football clubs reluctantly do this (2,4).
17 Lou, who was on the ball for Celtic and United (6).
19 Boat Race necessities (4).
20 List bets at Watford (8).
23 A cricket wag? (4,3).
24 Like Denis Law (5).
25 Test cricketer nicknamed Spiro (5).
26 The bell for a dangerous boxer? (5).

DOWN

2 A former Old Trafford but not Villa Park winger (5).
3 Head Canary at Carrow Road (3,5).
5 Where all boxers hope for a square deal (4).
6 The home of gridiron (7).
7 Throw Gill in to identify an ex-Test skipper (11).
8 The fastest Frenchman at the wheel (5).
9 United clubs, at Lancaster Gate for instance (11).
14 Basic soccer skill, but an art for Glenn Hoddle (4,4).
16 Fred, a racehorse trainer who sounded lovely (7).
18 Bramall Lane grass? (5).
21 Elizabeth Broome's married name (5).
22 He was no doubt just Edson to his mum (4).

ANSWERS

WHO DID WHAT? (Page 9): 1. Trevor Francis; 2. Chris Finnegan; 3. Keith Fletcher; 4. Emerson Fittipaldi; 5. Neale Fraser; 6. Dick Fosbury; 7. Joe Frazier; 8. Bryan Fletcher; 9. Tom Finney; 10. Brendan Foster.

11

4 THE TRIVIA TEST

See if you can select the right answer to each of these trivial sports questions. Award yourself one point for each correct answer.

Average score: 3   Greavsie: 4

1. Which former world heavyweight champion was once involved in a bar-room brawl in a South Wales pub?
a) Rocky Marciano; b) James J. Braddock; c) Ezzard Charles

2. Which outstanding British sportsman was the son of a Labour Member of Parliament?
a) Henry Cotton; b) Reg Harris; c) Fred Perry

3. Which father of identical twins scored goals at identical times in each half of an FA Cup Final?
a) Alan Taylor; b) Reg Lewis; c) Stan Mortensen

4. Which cricketer played in every Australian Test team captained by a Chappell— Ian and Greg?
a) Dennis Lillee; b) Allan Border; c) Rodney Marsh

5. Which golfer was first to have his portrait featured on a new issue of postage stamps in 1976?
a) Gary Player; b) Jack Nicklaus; c) Peter Thomson

6. Which 1966 World Cup hero became an undertaker when he retired from football?
a) George Cohen; b) Ray Wilson; c) Roger Hunt

7. Which England bowler was 'not out' as a batsman a record 55 times during his Test career?
a) Bob Willis; b) Brian Statham; c) Derek Underwood

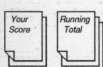
Your Score   Running Total

ANSWERS

ODD MAN OUT (Page 10): 1. Dick Richardson (did not win a British title); 2. Roger Bannister (did not win an Olympic gold medal); 3. Denis Law (did not play in the 1968 European Cup Final). 4. Denis Compton (did not captain England); 5. Joe Mercer (did not ride a Derby winner); 6. Gareth Edwards (was a scrum-half, not a fly-half).

5 SPORTS GRAM

Rearrange the letters to identify a team of 11 international footballers. We give a brief clue to help you. Award yourself one point for each correct answer.
Average score: 7   Greavsie 9

1. LOSE THE PRINT
He played in the 1969 FA Cup Final

2. SEVEN TRY GAS
He is at home at Goodison

3. RANK RAW LEMONS
He first made his mark with Preston

4. FAR FIVE LICK NET
He is the heart of the Welsh defence

5. LABOUR TRASH TIN
He might play for the Roundtable team

6. MOTHER BARS RAG
He spurs them on at Ibrox

7. BORN BOYS RAN
He started his career at The Hawthorns

8. LEND GOLD HEN
He passed with honours at London N.17.

9. KING LEAR RYE
He scored his early goals at Filbert Street

10. A NICE CHOIR SHALL
He could be expected to present goals at Christmas

11. I PROVE A CODE
He barrels down the wing for Rangers and Scotland

ANSWERS

SPORTSWORD (Page 11): ACROSS: 1 Banks; 4 Cream; 10 Luton; 11 Rangers; 12 In No Rush; 13 Dino; 15 Go Down; 17 Macari; 19 Oars; 20 Blissett; 23 Tail End; 24 Anglo; 25 Spiro; 26 Alarm. DOWN: 2 Aston; 3 Ken Brown; 5 Ring; 6 America; 7 Illingworth; 8 Prost; 9 Association; 14 Pass Ball; 16 Darling; 18 Blade; 21 Edgar; 22 Pele.

Your Score

Running Total

6 SPORTING CINEMA

Each question relates to sports-based films. One point for each correct answer.

Average score: 5
Greavsie: 6

1. Which former world middleweight boxing champion was played by Paul Newman in the film *Somebody Up There Likes Me?*
a) Jake LaMotta; b) Rocky Graziano; c) Carmen Basilio

2. Who played the part of double Olympic hero Jim Thorpe in *Man of Bronze?*
a) Burt Lancaster; b) Tony Curtis; c) Charlton Heston

3. Which AAA coach was the athletics consultant for the Oscar-winning *Chariots of Fire?*
a) Geoff Dyson; b) Ron Pickering; c) Tom McNab

4. In which film did Bobby Moore and Pele play supporting roles to Sylvester Stallone?
a) Escape to Victory; b) Go for Goal; c) The Big Shot

5. Which sport provides the background to *This Sporting Life*, starring Richard Harris and Rachel Roberts?
a) Motor Racing; b) Rugby League; c) Horse Racing

6. Who did Glenn Ford portray in the golfing biopic *Follow the Sun?*
a) Ben Hogan; b) Bobby Jones; c) Gene Sarazen

7. Who played the part of Angelo Dundee as supporting star to Muhammad Ali in *The Greatest?*
a) Burgess Meredith; b) Karl Malden; c) Ernest Borgnine

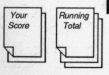

Your Score

Running Total

ANSWERS

THE TRIVIA TEST (Page 12): 1. Rocky Marciano (while stationed in South Wales with the US Army); 2. Fred Perry; 3. Reg Lewis (for Arsenal v Liverpool, 1950 Final); 4. Rodney Marsh; 5. Gary Player; 6. Ray Wilson; 7. Bob Willis.

7 TEAM SHEET

There are six famous football teams below, each with a key player missing. Award yourself one point for each absentee that you spot.
Average score: 3
Greavsie: 5

1. ENGLAND'S 1966 WORLD CUP WINNERS
Gordon Banks
George Cohen
Ray Wilson
Jack Charlton
Bobby Moore
Alan Ball
Roger Hunt
Bobby Charlton
Geoff Hurst
Martin Peters

2. CELTIC'S 1967 EUROPEAN CUP WINNERS
Ronnie Simpson
Jim Craig
Tommy Gemmell
Bobby Murdoch
Billy McNeill
John Clark
Jimmy Johnstone
Willie Wallace
Stevie Chalmers
Bobby Lennox

3. FOREST'S 1979 EUROPEAN CUP WINNERS
Peter Shilton
Larry Lloyd
Kenny Burns
Frank Clark
Trevor Francis
John McGovern
Ian Bowyer
John Robertson
Tony Woodcock
Garry Birtles

4. ARSENAL'S 1971 DOUBLE WINNERS
(FA Cup winning team)
Bob Wilson
Pat Rice
Bob McNab
Peter Storey
Frank McLintock
Peter Simpson
George Armstrong
John Radford
Ray Kennedy
Charlie George
Eddie Kelly (sub)

5. MAN UNITED'S 1977 FA CUP WINNERS
(FA Cup winning team)
Alex Stepney
Jimmy Nicholl
Arthur Albiston
Brian Greenhoff
Martin Buchan
Steve Coppell
Jimmy Greenhoff
Stuart Pearson
Lou Macari
Gordon Hill
Dave McCreery (s)

6. LIVERPOOL'S 1986 DOUBLE WINNERS
(FA Cup winning team)
Bruce Grobbelaar
Mark Lawrenson
Jim Beglin
Steve Nicol
Ronnie Whelan
Alan Hansen
Kenny Dalglish
Craig Johnston
Ian Rush
Kevin MacDonald
Steve McMahon (s)

ANSWERS

SPORTS GRAM (Page 13): 1. Peter Shilton; 2. Gary Stevens; 3. Mark Lawrenson; 4. Kevin Ratcliffe; 5. Arthur Albiston; 6. Graham Roberts; 7. Bryan Robson; 8. Glenn Hoddle; 9. Gary Lineker; 10. Charlie Nicholas; 11. Davie Cooper.

Your Score

Running Total

8 GUESS THE GUEST

*See how quickly you can identify
a star sportsman from the clues.*
Average score: 6   Greavsie: 8

For 12 points: Our mystery guest was born in Lancashire in 1952, and captained England at his sport from 1978 until 1982.

For 10 points: Skipper of Fylde, he won the first of his international caps in 1975 and was an ever-present in the England team for 34 successive matches.

For 8 points: A powerful and heavily-built lock forward, he captained England for a record stretch of 21 internationals.

For 6 points: England won eleven of those matches and he was at the peak of his popularity when he was forced to retire because of injury.

For 4 points: The injury that finished his career came when he was captaining Lancashire against North Midlands in the 1982 County Championship final at Moseley.

For 2 points: His captaincy these days is confined to regular appearances on the TV sports quiz programme *A Question of Sport* in which he has developed a double act with Emlyn Hughes.

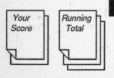

Your Score   Running Total

ANSWERS

SPORTING CINEMA (Page 14): 1. Rocky Graziano; 2. Burt Lancaster; 3. Tom McNab; 4. Escape to Victory; 5. Rugby League; 6. Ben Hogan; 7. Ernest Borgnine.

9 SPORTSTANGLE

Untangle the letters in each of the sections to identify famous sports personalities. Award yourself two points for each correct identification.

Average score: 6   Greavsie: 6

1. Clue: No doubt the cue ball suits him best.

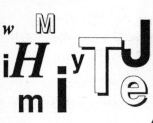

2. Clue: A toss of a coin could help you.

3. Clue: This should not throw you for long.

4. Clue: He is something of a flying Scot

ANSWERS

Your Score

Running Total

Each of the questions relate to sporting books. One point for each correct answer.
Average Score: 3
Greavsie: 4

10 SPORTS BOOKSHELF

1. Which motor racing driver had a book written about him called *All But My Life?*
a) Niki Lauda; b) John Surtees; c) Stirling Moss

2. *Ball of Fire* was title of the autobiography of which England cricketer?
a) John Snow; b) Fred Trueman; c) Bob Willis

3. *Mighty Mouse* featured which Rugby Union star?
a) Ian McLauchlan; b) JPR Williams; c) Ted Woodward

4. *The Gentle Giant* was the story of which footballer?
a) John Charles; b) Frank Swift; c) Roy McFarland

5. Who was the former world heavyweight champion featured in the book, *Victory Over Myself?*
a) Jersey Joe Walcott; b) Floyd Patterson; c) Ingemar Johansson

6. Hunter Davies spent a season with which football club for his book, *The Glory Game?*
a) Tottenham; b) Liverpool; c) Manchester United

7. Which cricketer's autobiography was titled *Cricket Through the Covers?*
a) Peter May; b) Cyril Washbrook; c) Tom Graveney

8. *My Life and Game* tells the story of which former Wimbledon lawn tennis champion?
a) Rod Laver; b) Bjorn Borg; c) Arthur Ashe

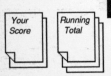

Your Score

Running Total

ANSWERS

GUESS THE GUEST (Page 16): The mystery personality is Bill Beaumont, former England Rugby Union captain and now a popular television personality.

11 THE NAME GAME

EACH clue leads to a well-known name. Put the initials in the appropriate squares to identify a sports star: One point for each correct answer, plus a bonus of five points for completing the main name.

Average score: 5 Greavsie: 11

1	2	3	4	5				
6	7	8	9	10	11	12	13	14

4 & 8	He skippered England and Leicestershire and has managed Yorkshire.
12 & 9	The Tonypandy lionheart who gave Joe Louis his hardest title defence.
10 &14	This Australian beat Jaroslav Drobny to win the 1952 Wimbledon title.
3 & 5	A kingsize Scot who captained Liverpool in the 1965 FA Cup Final.
7 &13	He has had all-round success with New Zealand and Nottinghamshire.
11 & 1	This Luton schoolteacher was the 1974 European marathon champion.
2 & 6	Billy Bremner succeeded him as manager of Leeds United.

ANSWERS

Your Score

Running Total

12
ON A
PLATE

Here are 15 easy questions to help you boost your score. Award yourself a point for each correct answer, plus a one point bonus every time that you get three successive questions right.
Average score: 12   Greavsie: 17

1. Which team is at home at Anfield?

2. Who took the world heavyweight title from Sonny Liston?

3. With which League club did Gary Lineker start his career?

4. Which bowler has taken most Test wickets?

5. How many times did Lester Piggott win the Derby?

6. Who ended Bjorn Borg's winning run at Wimbledon?

7. In which event was John Walker an Olympic champion?

8. Which horse won the 1987 Grand National?

9. With which sport do you associate the name Babe Ruth?

10. On which ground do Scotland play home Rugby matches?

11. Who rode Sportsman to many show jumping honours?

12. What nationality is footballer Oleg Blokhin?

13. At which sport was Reg Harris a world champion?

14. In which event did Al Oerter win four Olympic gold medals?

15. David Wilkie specialised in which swimming stroke?

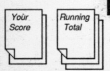

Your Score	Running Total

ANSWERS

SPORTS BOOKSHELF (Page 18): 1. Stirling Moss; 2. Fred Trueman; 3. Ian McLauchlan; 4. John Charles; 5. Floyd Patterson; 6 Tottenham; 7. Tom Graveney; 8. Bjorn Borg.

13 SPORTS SQUARE

The answers in this Sports Square overlap. Award yourself one point for each correct answer and a five-point bonus if you complete the square.

Average score: 14
Greavsie: 22

1a: Athletic footballing brothers (8)
1d: Did he amble to a boxing title? (7)
2a: A burden that batsmen enjoy (3)
3d: Sew on the medals for a Berlin hero (5)
7d: You may gather it is a road race (5)

4a: Half a hero in the wrestling ring? (6)
5d: A club that is now rich (7)
6d: Prompt demise in the play-offs (6)
8d: Just a short shot to the green (4)
14d: A tennis master in super Ryde (5)

9a: Fan lied to get into this ground (7)
10a: Derek Randall has done it well (7)
13d: A bubbling First Division boss I5)
16a: It comes in relays before wickets (3)
17a: You might stick to them at Bisley (4)

11a: A family enriched by Bill and John (6)
12d: This Law was king of Manchester (5)
15d: He was Leicester City's FA Cup captain (4)
18a: Her rags for a Derby winner (7)
19a: Player who could turn rivals gray (4)

ANSWERS

THE NAME GAME (Page 19): Welsh snooker star TERRY GRIFFITHS (Ray Illingworth, Tommy Farr, Frank Sedgman, Ron Yeats, Richard Hadlee, Ian Thompson, Eddie Gray).

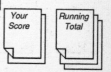

Your Score

Running Total

14 BEHIND THE WHEEL

Award yourself one point for each correct answer to these motor racing questions.
Average score: 4
Greavsie: 5

1. Which car was Graham Hill driving when he won the world championship in 1962?
a) Lotus; b) BRM; c) Cooper-Climax

2. How many times was Scotland's Jackie Stewart world motor racing champion?
a) Two; b) Three; c) Four

3. What nationality was South American driving master Juan-Manuel Fangio?
a) Brazilian; b) Colombian; c) Argentinian

4. Which car manufacturer has won most world championships?
a) Ferrari; b) Lotus; c) Maserati

5. In which country is the Zandvoort Grand Prix circuit?
a) Belgium; b) Holland; c) West Germany

6. Over how many miles is the Indianapolis 200 lap race staged?
a) 500; b) 750; c) 1000

7. Which driver holds the record for most victories in the British Grand Prix?
a) Stirling Moss; b) James Hunt; c) Jim Clark

8. Who was runner-up to Nigel Mansell in the 1987 British Grand Prix?
a) Nelson Piquet; b) Ayrton Senna; c) Alain Prost

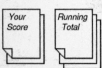

Your Score   Running Total

ANSWERS

ON A PLATE (Page 20): 1. Liverpool; 2. Cassius Clay (Muhammad Ali); 3. Leicester City; 4. Ian Botham; 5. Nine times; 6. John McEnroe; 7. 1,500 metres; 8. Maori Venture; 9. Baseball; 10. Murrayfield; 11. David Broome; 12. Russian; 13. Cycling; 14. Discus; 15. Breast-stroke.

15 ALL ★ AMERICAN

*There are 7 questions here about the American
sports scene. A point for each correct answer.*
Average score: 3   Greavsie: 4

1. Which city hosted the first Olympics to be staged in the
United States?

   a) Los Angeles; b) Chicago; c) St. Louis

2. Who holds the record for most touchdowns in a season in
professional American Football?

   a) John Riggins; b) Jim Brown; c) Walter Payton

3. In 1985, which basbeball star broke Ty Cobb's 57-year-old
record for most base hits in a career?

   a) Pete Rose; b) Hank Aaron; c) Rick Henderson

4. Which team has won most National Basketball Association
titles (16 between 1957 and 1986)?

   a) Boston Celtics; b) Detroit Pistons; c) Los Angeles Lakers

5. With which popular American sport do you associate the
name of top money earner Earl Anthony?

   a) Pool; b) Tenpin Bowling; c) Drag racing

6. In which State is the annual U.S. Masters golf tournament
staged?

   a) Georgia; b) Texas; c) Alabama

7. Which American track hero set six world records in one after-
noon during a meet at Michigan?

   a) Carl Lewis; b) Bobby-Joe Morrow; c) Jesse Owens

ANSWERS

SPORTS SQUARE (Page 21): ACROSS: 1 Charlton; 2 Ton; 4 Nelson;
9 Anfield; 10 Fielded; 11 Edrich; 16 Leg; 17 Guns; 18 Shergar; 19 Gary.
DOWN: 1 Carnera; 3 Owens; 5 Norwich; 6 Sudden; 7 Rally; 8 Chip;
12 Denis; 13 Lyall; 14 Perry; 15 Nish.

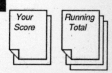

Your
Score

Running
Total

16
WHAT'S HIS NAME...?

There are 20 sportsmen on this page labelled only by their nickname. Award yourself one point for each correct identification.
Average score: 13
Greavsie: 16

1. Manassa Mauler (Boxing)

2. Wizard of Dribble (Football)

3. The Refrigerator (American Football)

4. Puff Puff (Athletics) 5. Brylcreem Boy (Cricket)

6. Dracula (Snooker) 7. Rockhampton Rocket (Tennis)

8. Nijinsky (Football) 9. The Raging Bull (Boxing)

10. Long Fella (Horse Racing) 11. Crafty Cockney (Darts)

12. Flying Finn (Athletics) 13. The Stilt (Basketball)

14. Big Bird (Cricket) 15. Lion of Vienna (Football)

16. The Shifter (Athletics) 17. The Walrus (Golf)

18. Ghost With A Hammer In His Hand (Boxing)

19. Pine Tree (Rugby Union) 20. Arkle (Cricket)

Your Score

Running Total

ANSWERS

BEHIND THE WHEEL (Page 22): 1. BRM; 2. Three; 3. Argentinian; 4. Ferrari; 5. Holland; 6. 500 miles; 7. Jim Clark (five victories, 1962-65 and 1967, all in Lotus cars); 8. Nelson Piquet.

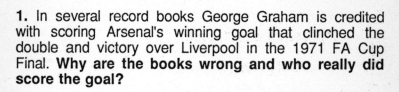

Here are four sporting mysteries for you to solve. Award yourself two points for each correct answer.
Average score: 2   Greavsie: 4

1. In several record books George Graham is credited with scoring Arsenal's winning goal that clinched the double and victory over Liverpool in the 1971 FA Cup Final. **Why are the books wrong and who really did score the goal?**

2. Jack Dempsey knocked Jess Willard down seven times in the first round of their 1919 world title fight and left the ring thinking the referee had stopped the contest. But nobody had heard the bell and Dempsey was recalled to continue the fight. He eventually won in the third round. The mystery is: **Why didn't Dempsey get a penny for his victory?**

3. Harry Bradshaw was beaten by Bobby Locke in a play-off for the British Open golf championship at Sandwich in 1949. **How did a beer bottle cost him outright victory?**

4. Dennis Lillee played four balls against Ian Botham and scored three runs during the first Test between Australia and England at Perth in December, 1979. There was then a long argument that finished with Lillee throwing his bat in anger. **What made Lillee lose his temper?**

ANSWERS

ALL AMERICAN (Page 23): 1. St. Louis (1904) ; 2. John Riggins (Washington Redskins); 3. Pete Rose (4,204 career base hits); 4. Boston Celtics; 5. Tenpin Bowling; 6. Jesse Owens (100 yards, long jump, 220 yards and 200 metres, 220 yards and 200 metres low hurdles - in the space of 45 minutes in 1935).

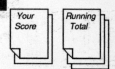

Your Score

Running Total

18 HARK WHO'S TALKING

There are quotes on this page from six famous sports personalities. Score one point for each that you correctly identify.
Average score: 2 Greavsie: 3

1. "Now that I've retired I mean to take it pretty easy, but I don't intend to be just the name above three green-grocer's shops."
a) George Best; b) Henry Cooper; c) Bob Willis

2. "This game either drives you to drink or the mad-house. Well I'm not ready for the madhouse, so I'll have another large one."
a) Tommy Docherty; b) Ron Atkinson; c) John Bond

3. "They could throw cushions and coins, specially coins, onto the court. It wouldn't upset me. Winning is the only important thing."
a) Martina Navratilova; b) Maria Bueno; c) Billie-Jean King

4. "My first priority is to finish motor racing above not below the ground."
a) Stirling Moss; b) James Hunt; c) Jackie Stewart

5. "I once shot a wild elephant in Africa. It was charging towards me and dropped dead at my feet. I wasn't a bit scared, but a four foot putt scares me to death."
a) Sam Snead; b) Ben Hogan; c) Bobby Locke

6. "When I see an action replay of the save on television I say, 'That's not on. He won't save that.' I don't know how I did."
a) Peter Shilton; b) Gordon Banks; c) Jim Montgomery

Your Score

Running Total

Do you know your way around the sports world? This will test you. One point each time you know where you are. **Average score: 6 Greavsie: 8**

19 GOING PLACES

Where are you when you're watching...

1. League football at Gay Meadow

2. County cricket at Grace Road

3. The St Leger

4. A motor racing Grand Prix at the Anderstorp circuit

5. World championship boxing at Kelvin Hall

6. The US Open golf championship at Pebble Beach

7. Lawn Tennis at Stade Roland Garros

8. A Rugby Union international at Lansdowne Road

9. World Championship snooker at The Crucible

10. Grand Prix motor cycling at Francorchamps

11. Yachting at Cowes

12. International football at the Maracana Stadium

ANSWERS

SPORTING MYSTERIES (Page 25): 1. ITV cameras proved that Eddie Kelly scored the goal; 2. Dempsey had bet his entire purse on his winning in the first round; 3. A Bradshaw drive ended in the neck of a broken beer bottle and he had to play 'as it lay.' 4. Lillee was told he could not play with his outlawed bat that was made of aluminium.

Your Score

Running Total

20 TEE TIME

You score a point for each correct answer in this round of golfing questions
Average score: 4 Greavsie 5

1. On which course did Jack Nicklaus beat Doug Sanders in a play-off for the British Open in 1970?
a) Royal Birkdale; b) St Andrews; c) Carnoustie

2. Which was the one major championship that eluded the great Sam Snead?
a) US Open; b) US Masters; c) British Open

3. Who has been the oldest post-war winner of the British Open championship?
a) Henry Cotton; b) Roberto de Vicenzo; c) Bobby Locke

4. How many times has Jack Nicklaus won the US Masters title?
a) Six; b) Seven; c) Eight

5. The British Open record aggregate of 268 for 72 holes is held by which golfer?
a) Jack Nicklaus; b) Arnold Palmer; c) Tom Watson

6. Which golfer has played for Britain a record ten times in the Ryder Cup?
a) Dai Rees; b) Max Faulkner; c) Christy O'Connor

7. Who holds the record for winning 18 tournaments in one season?
a) Ben Hogan; b) Bobby Jones; c) Byron Nelson

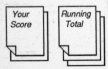

Your Score

Running Total

ANSWERS

HARK WHO'S TALKING (Page 26): 1. Henry Cooper; 2. Tommy Docherty; 3. Billie-Jean King; 4. James Hunt; 5. Sam Snead; 6. Gordon Banks (when discussing his famous save against Pele in the World Cup Finals in Mexico).

We have made 8 deliberate mistakes in the following summary about Olympic gymnastics, two in each paragraph. Underline each error as you discover it, and award yourself one point for each one that you find.
Average score: 3
Greavsie: 4

21 GYM SLIPS

1: Olga Korbut, an elf-like Rumanian who was 17 but looked 12, popularised gymnastics with her breath-taking performances in the 1972 Tokyo Olympics.

2: Olga was overshadowed in the Moscow Games four years later by Bulgarian Nadia Comaneci, the ballerina of the beam, who became the first gymnast to achieve a perfect score in Olympic competition. Nelli Kim, of the Soviet Union, also achieved perfect 10-out-of-10 marks during the 1976 Games.

3: Vera Caslavska, of Czechoslovakia, has won most individual Olympic gold medals with nine in the Games of 1964 and 1968. She won the hearts of the Mexican spectators in 1968 by performing her bar routine to the music of the Mexican Hat Dance.

4: Japan have won the women's title a record eight times (from 1952 to 1980). Including team events, the most successful gymnast in the history of the Olympics has been Russian Melissa Latynina, who amassed a record total of 18 medals from 1956 to 1964 - nine gold, five silver and four bronze.

ANSWERS

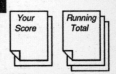

Your Score | Running Total

There are three sets of six questions on tennis here. Award yourself one point for each correct answer and a bonus of five points if you get at least four right in each set. **Average score: 9   Greavsie: 11**

FIRST SET

1. Who was the first left handed Wimbledon champion?
a) Jaroslav Drobny; b) Norman Brookes; c) Neale Fraser
2. Which country has won the Davis Cup most times?
a) Australia; b) France; c) USA
3. In which year did Arthur Ashe become US Open champion?
a) 1968; b) 1969; c) 1970
4. How many times was Bjorn Borg Wimbledon champion?
a) Four; b) Five; c) Six
5. Which Wimbledon star was a world table tennis champion?
a) Fred Perry; b) Jean Borotra; c) Budge Patty
6. Which great champion was nicknamed 'Little Wonder'?
a) Alice Marble; b) Lottie Dodd; c) Suzanne Lenglen

SECOND SET

1. Who was the first player to complete the Grand Slam?
a) Rod Laver; b) Jack Kramer; c) Donald Budge
2. Jaroslav Drobny was an Olympic medallist in which sport?
a) Ice Hockey; b) Judo; c) Soccer
3. In which year did John McEnroe win his first Wimbledon title?
a) 1982; b) 1981; c) 1983
4. How many times was Maureen Connolly Wimbledon champion?
a) Three; b) Four; c) Five
5. Which British tennis star is the daughter of an Archdeacon?
a) Jo Durie; b) Sue Barker; c) Virginia Wade
6. Which great champion was nicknamed 'Muscles'?
a) Ken Rosewall; b) Pancho Gonzales; c) Stan Smith

THIRD SET

1. Who was the first woman to complete the Grand Slam?
a) Margaret Smith; b) Maureen Connolly; c) Louise Brough
2. Althea Gibson was world class at which other sport?
a) Golf; b) Fencing; c) Hockey
3. In which year was Stan Smith Wimbledon champion?
a) 1971; b) 1973; c) 1972
4. How many times was Rod Laver Wimbledon champion?
a) Three; b) Four; c) Five
5. Which tennis star was the son of a high court judge?
a) Lew Hoad; b) John Newcombe; c) Neale Fraser
6. Who was nicknamed 'The Cat'?
a) Rafael Osuna; b) Alex Olmedo; c) Pancho Segura

ANSWERS

Your Score

Running Total

TEE TIME (Page 28): 1. St Andrews; 2. US Open; 3. Roberto de Vicenzo (44); 4. Six times; 5. Tom Watson; 6. Christy O'Connor; 7. Byron Nelson.

23 SEARCH FOR A CHAMP

How many world heavyweight boxing champions can you find in this grid? There are 15 names. Some appear in straightforward, left-to-right formations, others are printed in reverse or diagonally across the page. Award yourself one point for each name that you find. **Average score: 10   Greavsie 12**

W	J	O	H	N	S	O	N	W	Z	D	A	V
H	P	A	T	T	E	R	S	O	N	E	I	V
O	T	K	R	E	I	Z	A	R	F	M	S	L
K	Y	W	L	I	S	T	O	N	A	P	N	E
W	R	A	R	Z	U	S	O	R	N	S	R	G
I	W	L	H	P	S	G	C	Z	F	E	U	N
L	Y	C	U	B	P	I	G	N	X	Y	B	I
L	M	O	Q	J	A	M	S	I	U	O	L	L
A	L	T	H	N	O	C	B	X	V	S	K	E
R	U	T	O	W	A	T	Q	A	I	J	A	M
D	S	P	I	N	K	S	G	F	E	O	I	H
L	K	C	O	D	D	A	R	B	S	R	Q	C
W	T	F	O	R	E	M	A	N	E	Z	E	S

ANSWERS

GYM SLIPS (Page 29): 1. Olga was Russian, not Rumanian; 1972 Olympics were in Munich; 2. 1976 Games were in Montreal; Nadia is Rumanian, not Bulgarian; 3. Vera Caslavska won a record 7 individual golds, not 9; it was the floor routine, not bar; 4. Russia, not Japan have won most women's titles; it's Larissa Latynina, not Melissa.

Your Score   Running Total

24. GRIDIRON GRILLING

Award yourself one point for each correct answer to these American Football questions.
Average score: 3
Greavsie: 4

1. Which quarterback gained a record 331 yards with his passing for San Francisco 49ers in the 1985 Super Bowl?
a) Joe Montana; b) Dan Marino; c) Joe Namath

2. With which team has Marcus Allen made his reputation as one of the greats of Gridiron?
a) Miami Dolphins; b) Dallas Cowboys; c) Los Angeles Raiders

3. Chicago Bears scored a record 46 points in Superbowl XX — against which team?
a) LA Rams; b) New York Giants; c) New England Patriots

4. Who in 1985 broke the long-standing NFL rushing record?
a) Walter Payton; b) Eric Dickerson; c) Roger Craig

5. For which team did Jim Brown score a career record 126 touchdowns?
a) Pittsburgh Steelers; b) New York Jets; c) Cleveland

6. Which team won a record 11 NFL titles between 1929 and 1967?
a) Chicago Cardinals; b) Green Bay Packers; c) Minnesota

7. Who made a record 106 pass receptions in 1984?
a) Art Monk; b) Dan Ross; c) Charley Pointer

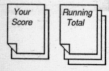

Your Score | Running Total

ANSWERS

25. THE FIVE STAR TEST

Award yourself one point for each correct identification in this five-star test.

Average score: 11 Greavsie: 18

1. Which five of these boxers won Olympic gold medals: Ingemar Johansson, Ray Robinson, Floyd Patterson, George Foreman, Nino Benvenuti, Tommy Hearns, Emile Griffith, Joe Frazier, Howard Davis, Roberto Duran.

2. Which five of these footballers scored FA Cup Final goals at Wembley: Luther Blissett, Norman Whiteside, Billy Bremner, Francis Lee, Trevor Brooking, Adrian Heath, Peter Osgood, Garth Crooks, Gordon McQueen, Peter Lorimer.

3. Which five of these batsman scored more than 7,000 Test runs: Jack Hobbs, Denis Compton, Greg Chappell, Don Bradman, Tom Graveney, Colin Cowdrey, Walter Hammond, Len Hutton, Garfield Sobers, Geoff Boycott.

4. Which five of these golfers have never won the British Open championship: Tom Weiskopf, Dai Rees, Tony Lema, Hale Irwin, Fred Daly, Bob Charles, Billy Casper, Johnny Miller, Byron Nelson, Hubert Green.

5. Which five of these tennis players have never won a Wimbledon singles title: Tony Roche, Ashley Cooper, Ilie Nastase, Dick Savitt, Jan Kodes, Fred Stolle, Roscoe Tanner, Vic Seixas, Ken Rosewall, Yvon Petra.

ANSWERS

SEARCH FOR A CHAMP (Page 31): 1. Johnson; 2. Patterson; 3.Dempsey; 4. Marciano; 5. Walcott; 6. Louis; 7. Willard; 8. Braddock; 9. Foreman; 10. Spinks; 11 Baer; 12. Schmeling; 13. Frazier; 14.Liston; 15 Burns

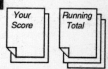

Your Score

Running Total

THE MARATHON MASTERS

Award yourself one point for each marathon master that you identify. The answers, but not in order, are Jim Peters, Rob de Castella, Abebe Bikila, Emil Zatopek, Alain Mimoun, Frank Shorter, Waldemar Cierpinski, Carlos Lopes

Average score: 4   Greavsie: 5

1. The galloping Czech who won the 1952 Olympic gold medal in his first ever marathon.

2. The Essex optician who collapsed 100 yards from the tape in the 1954 Empire Games marathon.

3. The former steeplechaser who won the Olympic marathon in 1976 and retained it in Moscow in 1980.

4. The man who clocked a world's best 2hr 7m 12s in Rotterdam in 1985.

5. The Australian nicknamed Deek who won the 1982 Commonwealth Games title.

6. The 1972 Olympic champion who won the gold medal in Munich, the city of his birth.

7. The first athlete to win two Olympic gold medals in the marathon.

8. The French-Algerian who won the 1956 Olympic marathon in Melbourne.

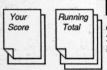

Your Score

Running Total

ANSWERS

The questions on this page all relate to the Derby. One point for each correct answer.
Average score: 5 Greavsie: 7

1. On which horse did Lester Piggott ride his first Derby winner at Epsom in 1954?
   a) Crepello; b) Never Say Die; c) St Paddy

2. Which jockey had his only Derby victory on Morston in 1973?
   a) Eddie Hide; b) George Moore; c) Neville Sellwood

3. Which trainer saddled 1981 winner Shergar?
   a) Michael Stoute; b) Vincent O'Brien; c) Ian Balding

4. The Minstrel was a winner for which owner?
   a) Aga Khan; b) Lord Halifax; c) Robert Sangster

5. Which was the first post-war odds-on winner?
   a) Nijinksky; b) Sir Ivor; c) Sea Bird 11

6. In which year was the Queen's horse Aureole runner-up?
   a) 1951; b) 1952; c) 1953

7. On which horse did Eddie Hide win the 1973 Derby?
   a) Morston; b) Blakeney; c) Charlottown

8. Which jockey had Derby wins on Tulyar and Hard Ridden?
   a) Harry Carr; b) Rae Johnstone; c) Charlie Smirke

ANSWERS

FIVE STAR TEST (Page 33): 1. Floyd Patterson, George Foreman, Nino Benvenuti, Joe Frazier, Howard Davis; 2. Norman Whiteside, Billy Bremner, Trevor Brooking, Garth Crooks, Gordon McQueen; 3. Greg Chappell, Colin Cowdrey, Walter Hammond, Garfield Sobers, Geoff Boycott; 4 Dai Rees, Hale Irwin, Billy Casper, Byron Nelson, Hubert Green; 5. Tony Roche, Ilie Nastase, Fred Stolle, Roscoe Tanner, Ken Rosewall.

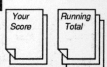

Your Score

Running Total

28 HARK WHO'S TALKING

There are quotes on this page from six more famous sports personalities. One point for each that you correctly identify.
Average score: 3 Greavsie: 4

1. "I felt confident from the moment Andy Pandy went at Becher's the second time around, leaving us in the lead. He is a joy to ride. You just have to sit up there and let him select the safest and quickest route."
a) Bryan Fletcher; b) Pat Taaffe; c) Tommy Stack

2. "When I lost the first three games against Nastase I wondered if I would be the first player to lose a Wimbledon final 6-0, 6-0, 6-0. Then I started to get my timing right and all my doubts disappeared."
a) Stan Smith; b) Jimmy Connors; c) Bjorn Borg

3. "As I stood on the 18th tee with Bob Charles I knew I had only to avoid the bunkers with my drive. I took a seven iron for my second and managed to toss the ball up within ten feet of the flag. That's when I knew I had the Open won."
a) Sandy Lyle; b) Tony Jacklin; c) Roberto de Vicenzo

4. "I'd give my right arm to get back into the England team. Well, you know what I mean..."
a) Peter Shilton; b) Ray Clemence; c) Gordon Banks

5. "The medals weigh more than I thought. It was hard to stand up straight when I had them all round my neck."
a) Carl Lewis; b) Teofilio Stevenson; c) Mark Spitz

6. "Football saved me from an ordinary life."
a) Jack Charlton; b) Rodney Marsh; c) Kevin Keegan

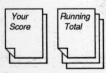

Your Score Running Total

ANSWERS

THE MARATHON MASTERS (Page 34): 1. Emil Zatopek; 2. Jim Peters; 3. Waldemar Cierpinski; 4. Carlos Lopes; 5. Rob de Castella; 6. Frank Shorter; 7. Abebe Bikila; 8. Alain Mimoun.

29

HOWZAT!

Imagine you are bowling a 6-ball over. But against who? Award yourself a point for each batsmen you identify from the clues.
Average score: 2 Greavsie: 4

1. This opener was the first professional to regularly captain England, and he scored 129 centuries. He led the England team that regained the Ashes in 1953.

2. Now we have an elegant left-handed batsman who scored 21 Test centuries for Australia. He played for Victoria and News South Wales and was the youngest member of Bradman's famous 1948 tourists.

3. Our third batsman is another left hander who had a brief spell as England captain. He stroked his way to 200 not out against India at Edgbaston in 1979.

4. A West Indian master comes in at number four. As a youngster he was suspended for two years for disputing a decision, but he has since emerged as a powerful strokemaker who in 1976 scored 1,710 Test runs - a record for a calendar year.

5. This all-rounder skippered Oxford University before playing for Worcestershire and then Sussex. A hard-hitting batsman, he is more highly regarded as a fast bowler, and has captained his country.

6. Finally, we have a wicket-keeper who is a capable, orthodox batsman. He was briefly captain of his County side and, with his County colleague Geoff Miller, rescued England in the fifth Test of the 1979 tour Down Under with a stand of 135.

ANSWERS

FIRST PAST THE POST (Page 35): 1. Never Say Die; 2. Eddie Hide; 3. Michael Stoute; 4. Robert Sangster; 5. Sir Ivor; 6. 1953; 7. Morston; 8. Charlie Smirke.

Your Score

Running Total

SPORTS NEWS EXTRA

30. HEADLINE MAKERS

Can you fill in the blanks in the following sporting headlines? Award yourself one point for each gap that you fill.

Average score: 8
Greavsie: 10

1.
BLANK KNOCKS OUT WALCOTT IN 13TH ROUND TO WIN TITLE

2.
PIGGOTT RIDES BLANK TO HIS NINTH DERBY VICTORY

3.
BLANK'S TWO GOALS CLINCH EUROPEAN CUP FINAL WIN FOR MAN UNITED

4.
BLANK BEATS SANDERS IN BRITISH OPEN PLAY-OFF AT ST ANDREWS

5.
BLANK PIPS KUTS TO WIN A THRILLER AT LONDON'S WHITE CITY

6.
BREMNER AND KEEGAN BOTH GET MARCHING ORDERS IN SEASON CURTAIN RAISER AT BLANK STADIUM

7.
BOWLER BLANK IS HIT FOR SIX SIZZLING SIXES BY SOBERS

8.
BILLY BOSTON SCORES HIS 500TH TRY FOR BLANK

9.
VIRGINIA CONQUERS BLANK TO WIN THE WIMBLEDON CENTENARY FINAL

10.
'WE WILL MAKE THE WEST INDIES GROVEL' SAYS SKIPPER BLANK

11.
COMPTON BOUNDARY CLINCHES ASHES WIN AT BLANK

12.
BLANK FIRST TO BEAT FOREMAN

13.
BLANK CLINCHES GOLD MEDAL ON FOXHUNTER

14.
HAT-TRICK FOR BLANK IN FA CUP FINAL

Your Score

Running Total

ANSWERS

31.

SECONDS OUT!

You have got to go 10 rounds with 10 different British boxers who all won world titles. Award yourself one point each time you can identify your opponent. Give yourself a five point knockout bonus if you can name 7 or more.
Average score: 5   Greavsie: 12

Round 1: This Welshman was known as the 'Little Atom' and was world champ for seven years from 1916.

Round 2: A skilful Scot, he became world bantam-weight king by outpointing Salvatore Burruni in 1966.

Round 3: Your featherweight opponent is a modern hero who dethroned Eusebio Pedroza.

Round 4: Now you're in against a southpaw who like fellow-Scot Ken Buchanan became world lightweight champion.

Round 5: Coming out from the light-welterweight corner is the 'Fighting Fireman' from Basildon.

Round 6: This Cockney ended the welterweight reign of Jose Napoles in Mexico City in 1975.

Round 7: Your light-middleweight opponent took the world title from Rocky Mattioli in 1979.

Round 8: The one and only 'Leamington Licker' comes out fighting for the middleweights.

Round 9: This former world light-heavyweight champion had two memorable battles with Gus Lesnevich.

Round 10: Finally, you are matched against the only British-born boxer to win the world heavyweight championship.

ANSWERS

HOWZAT (Page 37): 1. Len Hutton; 2. Neil Harvey; 3. David Gower; 4. Viv Richards; 5. Imran Khan; 6. Bob Taylor (who was briefly captain of Derbyshire).

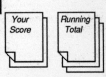

Your Score

Running Total

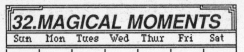

Sun	Mon	Tues	Wed	Thur	Fri	Sat

QUIZ OF THE YEAR

On the following pages we present a Quiz of the Year, recalling some of the greatest events in sporting history. All you have to do is select the correct year for each event. Greavsie said this test put years on him!

There are 120 events listed.
Average score: 58
Greavsie: 79

2nd.: Gene Fullmer, the Fighting Mormon, takes world middleweight title from Sugar Ray.
1953
1961
1957

4th.: Russian Prince Obolensky shatters the All Blacks with two wonder tries at Twickenham.
1936
1938
1930

5th.: Typhoon Tyson tears through Australia with 6 for 16 in a spell of just 51 balls.
1960
1955
1950

11th.: Steve Davis scores the first maximum 147 to be televised as he wins the Lada Classic.
1981
1982
1980

14th.: Walsall pull off one of the greatest of all FA Cup giant killings when they beat Arsenal 2-0.
1935
1933
1934

17th.: A record League crowd of 83,260 gathers at Maine Road to see Man United play Arsenal.
1948
1950
1952

19th.: Don Curry stops Colin Jones in four rounds in a world welterweight title defence.
1984
1985
1983

20th.: Millwall play Fulham at The Den in the first Football League match staged on a Sunday.
1974
1972
1970

22nd.: Foreman hammers Frazier in two rounds to win the world heavyweight championship.
1972
1973
1974

24th.: Six-goal Law finishes on losing side as Luton knock Manchester City out of the FA Cup.
1961
1963
1965

ANSWERS

SECONDS OUT (Page 39): 1. Jimmy Wilde; 2. Walter McGowan; 3. Barry McGuigan; 4. Jim Watt; 5. Terry Marsh; 6. John H. Stracey; 7. Maurice Hope; 8. Randolph Turpin; 9. Freddie Mills; 10. Bob Fitzsimmons.

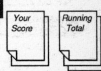

Your Score | Running Total

2nd.: Filbert Bayi holds off Walker and shatters 1500m world record in Commonwealth Games.
1978
1974
1970

3rd.: The Old Dancing Master Peter Jackson sinks Australia with last-minute try at Twickenham.
1956
1960
1958

6th.: Stanley Matthews, at 50, becomes the oldest League footballer, playing for Stoke v. Fulham.
1963
1964
1965

15th.: Ray Crawford torments Leeds as Colchester shock the FA Cup favourites.
1975
1973
1971

18th.: Jack 'Kid' Berg stops Mushy Callaghan to become world light-welterweight champion.
1930
1932
1934

19th.: Norwegian ice queen Sonja Henie wins first of her Olympic titles on the way to Hollywood!
1928
1932
1936

20th.: Ollie Campbell kicks all 21 points as Ireland sink the Scots to win the Triple Crown.
1980
1984
1982

23rd.: Canadian Burns, just 5ft 7in tall, outpoints Marvin Hart to become world heavyweight king.
1902
1910
1906

25th.: "I am the greatest!" roars Clay as he takes the world title from Sonny Liston.
1962
1964
1966

27th.: Garfield Sobers piles up the runs against Pakistan on his way to record 365 not out.
1958
1956
1954

ANSWERS

Your Score

Running Total

The answers for the QUIZ OF THE YEAR for February are on page 44

QUIZ OF THE YEAR — March

2nd. Basketball master Wilt Chamberlain scores 100 points in a single match.
1966
1964
1962

4th.: Third Division QPR beat First Division West Brom in the first League Cup Final at Wembley.
1965
1966
1967

8th.: Joe Frazier outpoints Muhammad Ali over 15 rounds in the 'Fight of the Century' in New York.
1971
1972
1973

15th.: Carleton goes over for three tries as England win the Calcutta Cup and clinch the Triple Crown
1976
1980
1978

16th.: Wanderers beat Royal Engineers 1-0 at The Kennington Oval in the first FA Cup Final.
1872
1882
1892

17th. Derek Randall strokes his way to 174 in the Centenary Test against Australia.
1975
1976
1977

20th.: Handy Andy Hancock races length of pitch for match-saving last-gasp try against Scotland.
1960
1955
1965

26th.: Kenny Dalglish wins his 100th cap and leads Scotland to a 3-0 win over Rumania.
1985
1986
1984

27th. Rangers v. Hibs draws 143,470 - a record for any British club match apart from cup finals.
1948
1952
1954

31st.: Red Rum overtakes Crisp on the run-in to win the Grand National for the first time.
1974
1973
1972

ANSWERS

QUIZ OF THE YEAR, January (Page 41): 2nd.: 1957; 4th.: 1936; 5th.: 1955; 11th.: 1982.; 14th.: 1933; 17th.: 1948; 19th.: 1985; 20th.: 1974; 22nd.: 1973; 24th.: 1961.

Your Score

Running Total

1st.: Walter Hammond wallops ten sixes on his way to an unbeaten 336 against New Zealand
1938
1933
1930

5th.: Jess Willard ends Jack Johnson's reign as world champion with a 26th round knockout win.
1910
1920
1915

8th.: Hammerin' Hank Aaron beats Babe Ruth's long-standing baseball home runs record.
1968
1974
1977

13th.: Joe Payne scores 10 goals for Luton against Bristol Rovers in a Third Division South match.
1936
1926
1946

15th.: England beat Scotland by a record 9-3 score-line in a Home Championship match.
1961
1959
1963

16th.: Malcolm Macdonald scores all of England's five goals against Cyprus at Wembley.
1977
1976
1975

18th.: Derby County outplayed as Bury score a record six goals in the FA Cup Final.
1914
1910
1903

25th.: Tiny Terry Allen outpoints Honore Pratesi to retain his world flyweight championship.
1950
1945
1955

26th.: Connors wins a record $500,000 for beating Newcombe in a Las Vegas challenge match.
1977
1975
1979

28th.: A crowd of 126,047 watch the first FA Cup Final at Wembley between Bolton and West Ham
1923
1921
1925

ANSWERS

Your Score

Running Total

5th.: Dixie Dean scores a hat-trick to beat Arsenal and reaches the 60-goals-in-a-season target.
1924
1932
1928

6th.: Roger Bannister becomes the first man to break the four-minute mile barrier.
1954
1953
1952

14th. Wakefield Trinity make it hell for Hull at Wembley with 38 points in the Challenge Cup Final.
1955
1960
1965

15th.: Rocky Marciano ko's Jersey Joe Walcott in the first round of his first world title defence.
1950
1947
1953

18th.: Real Madrid beat Eintracht Frankfurt 7-3 in a classic European Cup Final at Hampden Park.
1960
1962
1961

25th.: Celtic become the first British club to win the European Cup by beating Inter-Milan 2-1.
1965
1967
1963

27th.: Lawton and Mortensen score four each as England hammer Portugal 10-0 in Lisbon.
1947
1949
1951

28th.: Bob Appleyard takes 4 for 7 as New Zealand are skittled for an all-time Test low of 26.
1950
1960
1955

29th.: Emotional night for Matt Busby as Charlton leads Man United to European Cup Final win.
1968
1970
1969

31st.: Viv Richards hammers a record 189 not out in one day international at Old Trafford.
1985
1983
1984

ANSWERS

QUIZ OF THE YEAR, March (Page 43): 2nd.: 1962; 4th.: 1967; 8th.: 1971; 15th.: 1980; 16th.: 1872; 17th.: 1977; 20th.: 1965; 26th.: 1986; 27th.: 1948; 31st.: 1973

Your Score | Running Total

QUIZ OF THE YEAR — June

4th.: Aboyeur wins the Derby after a suffragette throws herself under the King's horse.
1907
1910
1913

7th. Banks makes miraculous save from Pele's header but is beaten by Jairzinho.
1970
1972
1974

8th. 'Enery's 'Ammer drops Clay but he is saved by the bell and wins in the fifth round.
1966
1963
1969

10th.: Sebastian Coe smashes world 800 metres record in Italy with a stunning 1m 41.73s run.
1981
1983
1979

16th. Holmes and Sutcliffe complete a world record opening stand of 555 for Yorkshire at Leyton
1932
1936
1934

17th.: Northern Ireland beat Czechoslovakia 2-1 to reach the World Cup quarter-finals.
1954
1958
1962

22nd.: Joe Louis knocks out James J. Braddock in the 8th round to become new world champion.
1937
1934
1939

23rd.: Patricia's Hope equals Mick the Miller record with second successive Derby victory.
1971
1975
1973

29th.: Pele, just 17, scores a wonder goal to help Brazil beat Sweden in the World Cup Final.
1954
1958
1962

30th.: England's footballers enjoy a goal rush Down Under as they annihilate Australia 17-0.
1951
1961
1971

Your Score

Running Total

ANSWERS

1st. Donald Budge beats Britain's Bunny Austin in straight sets to retain his Wimbledon title.
1938
1936
1934

4th.: West Germany beat favourites Hungary 3-2 to win the World Cup for the first time.
1950
1954
1958

6th.: Rod Laver retains his Wimbledon crown by beating Martin Mulligan in just 52 minutes.
1960
1969
1962

9th.: Watson beats Nicklaus by one shot with final round 65 in Turnberry thriller
1979
1977
1980

10th.: Randolph Turpin outpoints Sugar Ray Robinson to become world middleweight champion.
1951
1953
1949

12th.: Yorkshire spin ace Hedley Verity has Notts in knots as he takes all 10 wickets for 10 runs.
1938
1932
1928

24th. Dorando disqualified as Olympic officials help him across the line in London marathon.
1908
1912
1904

27th.: Steve Cram lowers world mile record to 3min. 46.32sec. in Oslo classic.
1985
1983
1984

30th.: Geoff Hurst's hat-trick clinches a World Cup victory for England against West Germany.
1962
1964
1966

31st.: Jim Laker finishes the fourth Test against the Aussies at Old Trafford with figures of 19 for 90!
1954
1956
1958

ANSWERS

QUIZ OF THE YEAR, May (Page 45): 5th.: 1928; 6th.: 1954; 14th.: 1960; 15th.: 1953; 18th.: 1960; 25th.: 1967; 27th.: 1947; 28th.: 1955; 29th.: 1968; 31st.: 1984.

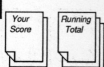

Your Score | Running Total

6th.: Gertrude Ederle becomes the first woman to swim the English Channel.
1926
1913
1920

7th.: Jim Peters collapses just short of victory in the Empire Games marathon in Canada.
1950
1954
1958

10th.: Dick Tiger knocks out Gene Fullmer in seven rounds to retain the world middleweight title.
1965
1963
1967

11th.: Don Bradman hits a record 309 runs on the first day of the Headingley Test against England.
1948
1937
1930

12th.: Goalkeeper Pat Jennings scores for Spurs against Manchester United at Old Trafford.
1963
1971
1967

18th. Fangio clinches his fifth world motor racing championship at the age of 46.
1957
1959
1961

21st.: Keith Peacock becomes the first substitute in League football for Charlton at Bolton.
1963
1965
1967

23rd.: Len Hutton scores world record 364 as England pile up 903 runs against Australia
1938
1937
1936

25th.: Captain Matthew Webb becomes the first man to swim the English Channel.
1885
1875
1880

31st.: Garfield Sobers slams six sixes in one over for Notts against Glamorgan at Swansea.
1962
1966
1968

ANSWERS

Your
Score

Running
Total

QUIZ OF THE YEAR, June (Page 46): 6th.: 1913; 7th.: 1970;
8th.: 1963;10th.: 1981; 16th.: 1932; 17th.: 1958; 22nd.: 1937;
23rd.: 1973; 29th.: 1958; 30th.: 1951.

3rd. Mary Peters strikes Olympic gold for Britain in the pentathlon.
1964
1968
1972

5th. John Petrie scores 13 goals as Arbroath beat Bon Accord 36-0 in a Scottish Cup tie.
1880
1885
1900

6th. Wilkie breaks the 2m 20s barrier with world record swim in the 200 metres breaststroke.
1973
1974
1975

10th.: Blackpool play Bolton Wanderers in the first Football League match to be televised.
1955
1965
1960

12th.: Young Scot Jackie Stewart roars to the first of his Grand Prix victories.
1961
1963
1965

15th. Scrum-half Jan Webster is man of the match as England beat the All Blacks in Auckland.
1978
1975
1973

16th.: Sugar Ray Leonard stops Thomas Hearns in 14th round to become undisputed champion.
1981
1982
1980

20th. Sweden's Gunder 'The Wonder' Haegg breaks the 14-minute barrier for 5,000 metres.
1932
1952
1942

22nd.: Gene Tunney outpoints Jack Dempsey in the 'Battle of the Long Count' in Chicago.
1927
1928
1929

28th. Ali hangs on to his title with a narrow points victory in third battle against Ken Norton.
1976
1972
1968

ANSWERS

QUIZ OF THE YEAR, July (Page 47): 1st.: 1938; 4th.: 1954; 6th.: 1962; 9th.: 1977; 10th.: 1951; 12th.: 1932; 24th.: 1908; 27th.: 1985; 30th.: 1966; 31st.: 1956.

Your Score   Running Total

1st.: Pele makes his farewell appearance for New York Cosmos against his old club Santos.

1977
1978
1979

2nd.: Larry Holmes forces Muhammad Ali to retire at the end of 10 rounds in Las Vegas.

1982
1978
1980

5th.: Clown Prince Len Shackleton scores 6 goals in his debut for Newcastle against Newport.

1956
1936
1946

6th.: 'Babe' Ruth scores record three home runs in one game as New York fans go wild.

1926
1930
1934

11th.: Spurs beat Everton 10-4 in Bill Nicholson's first match as manager.

1956
1958
1954

13th.: Dead-eye John Lowe wins £102,000 for 501 score with nine darts in world championships.

1982
1983
1984

18th.: Bob Beamon shatters the world long jump record with a leap of 8.90m (29ft 2.50in).

1968
1976
1972

21st.: Abebe Bikila retains Olympic marathon title and sets a new world best time.

1960
1964
1956

24th.: Derek Johnstone, at 16, becomes youngest Scottish League Cup finalist with Rangers.

1969
1970
1971

26th.: Rocky Marciano ends the career of Joe Louis by grounding the Brown Bomber in round 8.

1949
1950
1951

ANSWERS

Your Score

Running Total

4th.: Great Britain swamp New Zealand 53-19 in a World Cup Rugby League match in Paris.

1976
1974
1972

7th.: Henry Cooper wins a record third Lonsdale Belt outright by stopping Billy Walker.

1967
1965
1963

9th.: Jimmy White, 18, becomes youngest world amateur snooker champion in whirlwind style.

1980
1981
1982

11th.: Piggott wins on Karabas for his second successive Washington International triumph.

1971
1970
1969

17th.: 'Super' Snell lowers the world mile record to 3min 54.1sec in Auckland.

1960
1964
1962

20th.: Ted MacDougall scores a record 9 goals for Bournemouth in an FA Cup tie against Margate.

1969
1970
1971

25th.: Puskas leads the 'Magical Magyars' to a 6-3 victory over England at Wembley.

1955
1954
1953

26th.: Sugar Ray Leonard forces Roberto Duran to retire in the 8th round of their return title fight.

1978
1980
1982

29th.: Chris Brasher disqualified but then reinstated as the Olympic steeplechase gold medallist.

1956
1960
1952

30th.: First ever England-Scotland football international ends in a goalless draw.

1892
1882
1872

ANSWERS

QUIZ OF THE YEAR, September (Page 49): 3rd. 1972; 5th.: 1885;
6th.: 1973; 10th.: 1960; 12th.: 1965; 15th.: 1973; 16th.: 1981;
20th.: 1942; 22nd.: 1927; 28th.: 1976.

Your Score   Running Total

QUIZ OF THE YEAR December

3rd.: British-born Derek Clayton becomes first man to beat the 2 hours 10 minutes marathon barrier.
1965
1963
1967

6th.: John H. Stracey stops Jose Napoles in Mexico to win the world welterweight title.
1977
1975
1973

9th.: Spain's goalkeeper Zamora goes off in tears after England's seven-goal blitz at Highbury
1931
1935
1939

13th.: Wolves master Honved 3-2 at Molineux to become uncrowned kings of Europe.
1958
1956
1954

14th.: Ted Drake scores seven goals for Arsenal in a First Division match at Aston Villa.
1935
1930
1925

17th.: 'Ageless' Archie Moore becomes world light-heavyweight champion by beating Joey Maxim.
1950
1948
1952

21st.: Summers scores five as Charlton hit back from 5-1 to beat Huddersfield 7-6 at The Valley.
1947
1957
1967

26th.: Jack Johnson beats Tommy Burns to become the first black world heavyweight champion.
1907
1908
1909

27th. Normandy beats the 'unbeatable' Persian War in thrilling Irish Sweeps Hurdle race.
1969
1967
1965

31st.: Cowdrey scores his first century against the Aussies but England are all out for 191.
1952
1954
1956

ANSWERS

Your Score

Running Total

33 GUESS THE GUEST

*See how quickly you can identify
a star sportsman from the clues.*
Average score: 4   Greavsie: 8

For 12 points: Our mystery guest was born in Scunthorpe in 1944 and became a professional at his sport at the age of 17 after representing England boys in international matches.

For 10 points: At the start of his professional career he was based at Potters Bar in Hertfordshire.

For 8 points: In 1963 he competed in the British Open for the first time and finished in 30th position. The venue was Royal Lytham and St Annes.

For 6 points: It was at Royal Lytham that he had the greatest triumph of his career in 1969.

For 4 points: He became the first British winner of the Open since 1951. Within the year he had also won the US Open, and he remains the only British golfer ever to have held both championships at the same time.

For 2 points: Now based at the Sotogrande golf course on the Costa del Sol, he was the non-playing captain of the Ryder Cup team that beat the United States in 1985. He has become a respected BBCtv commentator.

ANSWERS

QUIZ OF THE YEAR, November (Page 51): 4th.: 1972; 7th.: 1967; 9th.: 1980; 11th.: 1969;   17th.: 1964; 20th.: 1971; 25th.: 1953; 26th.: 1980; 29th.: 1956; 30th.: 1872.

Your Score

Running Total

34

MORE ODD MEN OUT

Who is the odd man out in each of the following six lists? We give you a little 'think hint' to help. Award yourself one point for each correct answer.
Average score: 3 Greavsie: 4

1. British boxers Richard Dunn, Alan Minter, Jim Watt, Charlie Magri, Maurice Hope, Herol Graham, Jack Bodell. *Think styles.*

2. Football managers Don Revie, Ron Greenwood, Bob Paisley, Howard Kendall, Joe Mercer, Stan Cullis, Bill Nicholson. *Think championships.*

3. Marathon runners Abebe Bikila, Jim Peters, Alain Mimoun, Frank Shorter, Emil Zatopek, Waldemar Cierpinski, Carlos Lopes. *Think Olympics.*

4. Test cricketers Rodney Marsh, Bert Oldfield, Alan Knott, Godfrey Evans, John Waite, Hugh Tayfield, Jeff Dujon. *Think stumps.*

5. National Hunt jockeys Fred Winter, Dave Dick, Bryan Fletcher, Tommy Stack, Bob Champion, Pat Taaffe, Johnny Francome. *Think Nationals.*

6. Golfers Sam Snead, Ben Hogan, Fred Daly, Gene Littler, Max Faulkner, Kel Nagle, Bill Rogers. *Think British Opens.*

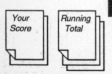

Your Score

Running Total

ANSWERS

35 THE TRIVIA TEST

See if you can select the right answer to each of these trivial sports questions. Award yourself one point for each correct answer.
Average score: 2 Greavsie: 3

1. Which former England cricket captain used to hum classical music to himself while at the batting crease?
a) Peter May; b) Ted Dexter; c) Mike Brearley

2. Which national leader was once given a trial as a baseball pitcher by a scout for the New York Giants?
a) Ronald Reagan; b) Pierre Trudeau; c) Fidel Castro

3. Which First Division club had ten players on international duty on 20 November 1974?
a) Liverpool; b) Leeds United; c) Manchester United

4. Which Olympic champion threw his gold medal into the Ohio River after being refused service in a 'whites only' restaurant?
a) Jesse Owens; b) Bob Beamon; c) Cassius Clay

5. Which battling, Pommy-bashing Aussie cricketer was known as 'Slasher'?
a) Ken Mackay; b) Keith Miller; c) Ian Redpath

6. Which golfer was the son of a gravedigger?
a) Doug Sanders; b) Lee Trevino; c) Ray Floyd

7. Which one of these footballers was trained as a slaughterman?
a) Ron Yeats; b) Ron Harris; c) Norman Hunter

ANSWERS

GUESS THE GUEST (Page 53): The mystery personality is golfer Tony Jacklin, the only British golfer ever to hold the British and American Open championships at one and the same time.

Your Score

Running Total

36 SPORTS GRAM

Rearrange the letters to identify 10 'golden oldie' sports stars. We give a brief clue to help. Award yourself one point for each correct answer.
Average score: 6 Greavsie 7

1. NO GENTS BARRIER
There have been miles of stories written about him

2. ROLL AND A PERM
He had an army of supporters

3. ROUGH NAILS ON BOAT
She struck gold in the pool

4. STOP EGG LITTER
You should race to this one!

5. MINCED ON TOPS
He was the cream of cricketers

6. SHY ON JET CAR
This ex-world boxing champion had a welter of talent

7. TEA IS IN SALE
A character who often kicked up a racket

8. WHY LAST TEAM NETS
He winged his way into the sporting history books

9. DRAW THE RED GAS
A Welsh idol who passed with flying colours

10. A CROOK IN MY CAR
Nobody ever got the better of him

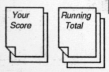

Your Score

Running Total

Each question relates to sports-based films. One point for each correct answer.
Average score: 4
Greavsie: 5

1. The Great White Hope is based on the life of which former world boxing champion?
a) Joe Louis; b) Jack Johnson; c) Ezzard Charles

2. Who played the title role in the biopic The Babe Ruth Story?
a)William Bendix; b) Spencer Tracy; c) Dana Andrews

3. In the film The Final Test, which actor played the part of the England captain?
a) Robert Donat; b) Robert Morley; c) Jack Warner

4. Which horse was featured in the film Champions that starred John Hurt?
a) Red Rum; b) Aldaniti; c) Devon Loch

5. Who was the former boxer who got into a clinch with Susan George in Mandingo?
a) Ken Norton; b) Buster Mathis; c) Ernie Terrell

6. Which sport provides the background to The Natural, starring Robert Redford?
a) American football; b) Baseball; c) Ice Hockey

7. Who played the leading role in the boxing biopic Raging Bull?
a) Al Pacino; b) James Caan; c) Robert DeNiro

ANSWERS

THE TRIVIA TEST (Page 55): 1. Mike Brearley; 2. Fidel Castro;
3. Leeds United; 4. Cassius Clay; 5. Ken Mackay; 6. Lee Trevino;
7. Ron Yeats.

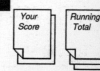

Your Score

Running Total

38 THE NAME GAME

EACH clue leads to a well-known name. Put the initials in the appropriate squares to identify a sports star: One point for each correct answer, plus a bonus of five points for completing the main name.

Average score: 4 Greavsie: 10

1	2	3	4	5				
6	7	8	9	10	11	12	13	14

2 & 12	A big puncher who was outpointed by Ali and who knocked down Holmes.
13 & 7	The Argentinian who has passed with honours at White Hart Lane.
5 & 10	This former World Cup referee blew the whistle on It's A Knockout.
8 & 3	A toothless tiger who was the hero of 1966 and all that.
11 & 14	The British driver who smashed the land speed record in Nevada in 1983.
9 & 1	The first black British boxing champion who had an even more famous brother.
4 & 6	This golfing great was the King of Swing and was nicknamed Slammin'.

Your Score

Running Total

ANSWERS

SPORTS GRAM (Page 56): 1. Roger Bannister; 2. Arnold Palmer; 3. Anita Lonsbrough; 4. Lester Piggott; 5. Denis Compton; 6. John Stracey; 7. Ilie Nastase; 8. Stanley Matthews; 9. Gareth Edwards;10. Rocky Marciano.

58

39
ON A
PLATE

Here are 15 easy questions to help you boost your score. Award yourself a point for each correct answer, plus a one point bonus every time you get three successive questions right.
Average score: 10   Greavsie: 13

1. Which team is at home at Roker Park?

2. Who took the world heavyweight title from Jersey Joe Walcott?

3. With which League club did Kevin Keegan start his career?

4. Which batsman has scored most Test runs?

5. How many times did Red Rum win the Grand National?

6. Who did Boris Becker beat in the 1985 Wimbledon final?

7. In which event did Lynn Davies win an Olympic gold medal?

8. On which horse did Walter Swinburn win the 1981 Derby?

9. With which sport do you associate the name Laszlo Papp?

10. On which ground do Ireland play home Rugby internationals?

11. Who won an Olympic silver medal on Psalm?

12. What nationality is marathon runner Carlos Lopes?

13. At which sport was Dave Starbrook world class?

14. In which event did Bob Mathias win two Olympic golds?

15. Judy Grinham specialised in which swimming stroke?

ANSWERS

SPORTING CINEMA (Page 57): 1. Jack Johnson; 2. William Bendix; 3. Jack Warner; 4. Aldaniti; 5. Ken Norton; 6. Baseball; 7. Robert DeNiro.

Your Score

Running Total

You have five minutes to answer each teaser.
You get one point for each correct answer and
a 5-point bonus each time you beat the clock.

40 BEAT THE CLOCK

Average score: 35 Greavsie: 46

1. Name the eight clubs that won the FA Cup during the 1960s.

2. Name Lester Piggott's nine Derby winners.

3. Name the eight opponents that Muhammad Ali (aka Cassius Clay) met more than once during his career.

4. Name the original twelve members of the Football League when it was formed in 1888.

5. Name the nine men who have managed Arsenal since the war.

Your Score

Running Total

ANSWERS

THE NAME GAME (Page 58): Javelin thrower TESSA SANDERSON (Earnie Shavers, Osvaldo Ardiles, Arthur Ellis, Nobby Stiles, Richard Noble, Dick Turpin, Sam Snead).

41 WHO'S WHO OF THE OLYMPICS

Here are 15 questions that will provide you with a Who's Who test of your knowledge of the greatest Olympic champions. One point for each correct answer.
Average score: 8
Greavsie: 11

1. Who holds the record for winning most individual gold medals (10) in men's events?
a) Mark Spitz (swimming); b) Ray Ewry (athletics); c) Eric Heiden (speed skating)

2. Who won four gold medals in the women's athletics in the 1948 Olympics in London?
a) Mildred Didrikson; b) Fanny Blankers-Koen; c) Shirley Strickland

3. Who is the runner who won nine gold and three silver medals in the Games of 1920, 1924 and 1928?
a) Ville Ritola; b) Erik Lemming; c) Paavo Nurmi

4. Who was the first boxer to win three Olympic gold medals?
a) Teofilio Stevenson; b) Oliver Kirk; c) Laszlo Papp

5. Who was the last cyclist to win three Olympic gold medals?
a) Daniel Morelon; b) Paul Masson; c) Robert Carpentier

6. Who is the rider who has won most gold medals (4) in the equestrian show jumping ring?
a) Richard Meade; b) Hans-Gunter Winkler; c) Raimondo d'Inzeo

Continued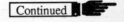

ANSWERS

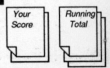

Your Score | Running Total

7. Who was the last figure skater to win three individual gold medals?
a) Gillis Grafstrom; b) Sonja Henie; c) Dick Button

8. Who was the Texan who won three gold medals on the track in the 1956 Melbourne Olympics?
a) Bobby-Joe Morrow; b) Harrison Dillard; c) Andy Stanfield

9. Who was the last men's Alpine skiier to win three Olympic gold medals?
a) Toni Sailer; b) Franz Klammer; c) Jean-Claude Killy

10. Who won the women's 100 metres freestyle at three successive Olympics?
a) Dawn Fraser; b) Barbara Krause; c) Kornelia Ender

11. Who was the British boxer who won two successive gold medals in the middleweight division?
a) Johnny Douglas; b) Chris Finnegan; c) Harry Mallin

12. Who is the only athlete to have won a gold medal in his event at four successive Olympics?
a) John Flanagan; b) Al Oerter; c) Parry O'Brien

13. Who was the triple gold medallist in rowing whose daughter became world famous?
a) John Kelly; b) Kurt Streep; c) Paul Hayworth

14. Who won five gold medals in the Olympic swimming pool and later became a Hollywood Tarzan?
a) Buster Crabbe; b) Bruce Bennett; c) Johnny Weissmuller

15. Who is the Russian who won 12 team and individual medals in the men's gymnastics?
a) Boris Shakhlin; b) Nikolai Andrianov; c) Viktor Chukarin

ANSWERS

BEAT THE CLOCK (Page 60): 1. Wolves (1960), Spurs (1961-62-67), Man. United (1963), West Ham (1964), Liverpool (1965), Everton (1966), West Brom (1968), Man City (1969). 2. Never Say Die, Crepello, St Paddy, Sir Ivor, Nijinksky, Roberto, Empery, The Minstrel, Teenoso. 3. Sonny Liston, Henry Cooper, Joe Frazier Jerry Quarry, Floyd Patterson, Ken Norton, Joe Bugner, Leon Spinks.

4. Accrington Stanley, Aston Villa, Blackburn Rovers, Bolton Wanderers, Burnley, Derby County, Everton, Notts County, Preston North End, Stoke, West Bromwich Albion, Wolves. 5. George Allison, Tom Whittaker, Jack Crayston, George Swindin, Billy Wright, Bertie Mee, Terry Neill, Don Howe, George Graham.

SPORTSWORD

Award yourself one point for each clue that you solve correctly plus a bonus of 10 points if you complete the crossword.

Average score: 16
Greavsie: 22

ACROSS

6 The Ohio Bear who is something of a green giant! (4,8).
8 An angler may use it catching tropical fish! (3,4).
9 There is a substitute for this in football (5).
10 David Bryant is not prejudiced when using it (4)
12 A dropped player hopes for one of these (6).
14 Perhaps Joe or his brother Gerry, who scored dozens of goals between them (5).
15 They are usually named with the runners (6).
16 Ballesteros at the short hole? (4).
19 Horses race round here like a dose of salts (4).
21 Ballyregan Bob is the prime example (4,3).
22 Match officials who have plenty of pluck? (4,8)

DOWN

1 Where sportsmen curl and hurl (8).
2 How an untrained athlete feels (5).
3 The space strikers find in races? (5).
4 Ian Botham's attire? (7)
5 Richard, who was lion-hearted against Ali (4).
6 Ashen Bjorn can identify this Liverpool star (4,6)
7 A champion faces them (10)
11 Indianapolis petrol? (3).
12 One on the snooker table (3).
13 They play at Pittodrie (8).
14 He collected the FA Cup at Wembley in 1972 (7).
17 Juventus made one that could not be refused when buying Ian Rush (5).
18 Cricket trophy remains? (5).
20 Medium pacers seem to use it a lot (4)

ANSWERS

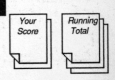

Your Score

Running Total

43 GUESS THE GUEST

*See how quickly you can identify
a star sportsman from the clues.*
Average score: 4 Greavsie: 10

For 12 points: Our mystery guest was born in Middlesbrough in 1935 and started his playing career as a junior with Great Broughton.

For 10 points: A centre-forward, he became a professional at Ayresome Park and later played at Roker Park.

For 8 points: He was a prolific goalscorer and won two full caps with England before a knee injury finished his career at the age of 28.

For 6 points: He switched to football management and started his new career in the basement of the Fourth Division with Hartlepool.

For 4 points: Along with his partner, Peter Taylor, he moved to Derby and steered them to the First Division championship in 1972. At 36, he was then the youngest ever manager of a League title winning team.

For 2 points: An outspoken character, he later managed Brighton and Leeds before taking over at Nottingham Forest with whom he has twice won the European Cup.

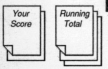

Your Score | Running Total

ANSWERS

WHO'S WHO OF THE OLYMPICS (Page 62): 7. Sonja Henie; 8. Bobby-Joe Morrow; 9. Jean-Claude Killy; 10. Dawn Fraser; 11. Harry Mallin; 12. Al Oerter; 13. John Kelly (whose daughter was Grace Kelly); 14. Johnny Weissmuller; 15. Nikolai Andrianov.

44 SPORTSTANGLE

Untangle the letters in each of the sections to identify famous sports personalities. Award yourself two points for each correct identification.

Average score: 4 Greavsie: 6

---

1. Clue: He used to win aerial battles by a neck

N A T c R J
a c
o H K L

---

2. Clue: This athlete sounds a colourful type

r B K
r C G
E L a o

---

3. Clue: He has enjoyed many marvellous wins.

R H
e A a M
R L
i G N V

---

4. Clue: She provided a winning service.

V Y o
c W L a n
n e E E

ANSWERS

SPORTSWORD (Page 63): ACROSS: 6 Jack Nicklaus; 8 Hot Line; 9 Bench; 10 Bias; 12 Recall; 14 Baker; 15 Riders; 16 Seve; 19 Epsom; 21 Fast Dog; 22 Game Referees. DOWN: 1 Scotland; 2 Unfit; 3 Acres; 4 Clobber; 5 Dunn; 6 John Barnes; 7 Challenges; 11 Gas; 12 Red; 13 Aberdeen; 14 Bremner; 17 Offer; 18 Ashes; 20 Seam.

Your Score

Running Total

65

45 SPORTS BOOKSHELF

1. Which motor racing driver had a book written about him called *Against All Odds?*
a) James Hunt; b) Jackie Stewart; c) John Surtees

2. *Soccer My Battlefield* was the title of the autobiography of which England footballer?
a) Norman Hunter; b) Nobby Stiles; c) Alan Mullery

3. *My Bleeding Business* featured which boxer?
a) Chris Finnegan; b) Henry Cooper; c) Terry Downes

4. Who tells his story in *I Don't Bruise Easily?*
a) Graham Roberts; b) Brian Close; c) Bill Beaumont

5. Which golfer is featured in the book *Go For Broke?*
a) Lee Trevino; b) Johnny Miller; c) Arnold Palmer

6. Which footballer headed a chapter, *'What Directors Know About the Game'* and left it blank?
a) Raich Carter; b) Len Shackleton; c) Tommy Docherty

7. *Behind the Stumps* was the autobiography of which Kent and England wicket keeper?
a) Alan Knott; b) Leslie Ames; c) Godfrey Evans

8. *Portrait in Motion* tells of a year in the life of which lawn tennis champion?
a) Arthur Ashe; b) Ken Rosewall; c) Ilie Nastase

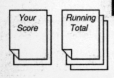

Your Score

Running Total

ANSWERS

GUESS THE GUEST (Page 64): The mystery personality is Brian Clough, manager of Nottingham Forest and former England centre-forward who scored 251 League goals in just 275 matches.

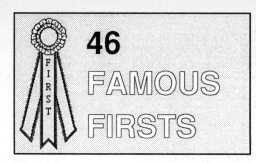

FAMOUS FIRSTS

How many of these pioneering record breakers can you identify? Award yourself one point for each correct name.
Average score: 5
Greavsie 8

WHO WAS THE FIRST MAN TO...

1…break the 3mins 50sec. mile barrier in athletics?

2…be sold for more than £100,000 in an all-British football transfer?

3...win three successive British Open titles in post-war golf?

4…take 300 wickets in Test cricket?

5…regain the world heavyweight boxing championship?

6…score a maximum 147 in a world championship snooker match?

7…retain the 5,000 metres title in Olympic athletics?

8…train three successive post-war winners in the Grand National?

9…score 60 Football League goals in a single season?

10…to score a century of centuries in post-war cricket?

ANSWERS

SPORTSTANGLE (Page 65): 1. Jack Charlton; 2. Roger Black;
3. Marvin Hagler; 4. Evonne Cawley.

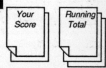

Your Score | Running Total

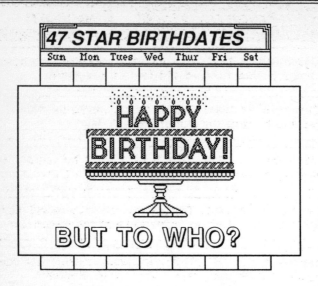

47 STAR BIRTHDATES

Sun	Mon	Tues	Wed	Thur	Fri	Sat

HAPPY BIRTHDAY!

BUT TO WHO?

On the following pages we present the birthdates and star signs of 120 prominent sports personalities of the past and present. Award yourself one point for each one that you can identify.

Average score: 54
Greavsie: 71

1. **December 24 1932:** This ex-Kent cricketer was born in India and played a record 114 Tests for England.

2. **December 27 1931:** This ex-Leeds footballer played for Wales and became the idol of Turin.

3. **December 28 1939:** This Scot started his career with Leicester and captained Arsenal's 1970-71 'double' side.

4. **December 29 1881:** This boxer took the world heavyweight title from Jack Johnson and was the tallest champ.

5. **December 30 1937:** This goalkeeper started his career with Chesterfield and played 73 times for England.

6. **January 1 1922:** This world middleweight champion won and lost the title in fights with Tony Zale.

7. **January 4 1935:** This world heavyweight champion was managed by the man who moulded Mike Tyson.

8. **January 6 1945:** This Welsh fly-half was known as 'The King' and had a prolific partnership with Gareth Edwards.

9. **January 16 1941:** This tennis star was the darling of Wimbledon and runner-up to Angela Mortimer in 1961.

10. **January 17 1942:** This boxer was Olympic light-heavy champion in 1960 and lost 5 of 61 professional fights.

ANSWERS

FAMOUS FIRSTS (Page 67): 1 John Walker; 2 Alan Ball; 3 Peter Thomson; 4 Fred Trueman; 5 Floyd Patterson; 6 Cliff Thorburn; 7 Lasse Viren; 8 Vincent O'Brien; 9 Dixie Dean; 10 Tom Graveney.

Your Score

Running Total

STAR BIRTHDATES — Aquarius

1. **January 21 1940:** This golfer was born in Ohio and has won a record 20 major championships.

2. **January 23 1919:** This former football manager guided Liverpool to three European Cup Final triumphs.

3. **January 31 1914:** This boxer became the oldest heavyweight champion when he knocked out Ezzard Charles.

4. **February 1 1915:** This footballer started with Stoke at the age of 17 and finished with them at 50.

5. **February 2 1942:** This goalkeeper captained the 1982 World Cup winners in Spain.

6. **February 6 1931:** This fiery fast bowler took his 300th Test wicket for England in 1964.

7. **February 10 1940:** This all-rounder struck gold in the 1964 Olympics when she beat the world long jump record.

8. **February 11 1934:** This British speed ace was world champion on two and four wheels.

9. **February 14 1951:** This footballer started his career with Scunthorpe and finished it at St James's Park.

10. **February 16 1959:** This German-born tennis star was Wimbledon men's runner-up in 1982.

ANSWERS

Your Score

Running Total

The Aquarius Star Birthday answers are on page 72.

70

1. **February 21 1937: This Australian athlete held seven world running records at the same time in the 1960s.**

2. **February 22 1949: This motor racing ace was born in Vienna and was world champion for the first time in 1975.**

3. **February 24 1940: This footballer was Scotland's top goalscorer when at Maine Road and Old Trafford.**

4. **February 28 1938: This Cockney was 1956 Olympic fly-weight champion and was a professional nine-stone king.**

5. **March 1 1940: This showjumper has had many success-ful horses including Sunsalve, Philco and Mister Softee.**

6. **March 4 1951: This Scot scored the winning goal for Liverpool in the 1978 European Cup Final.**

7. **March 7 1952: This cricketer was born in Antigua and succeeded Clive Lloyd as West Indies captain.**

8. **March 11 1923: This tennis player won four women's singles titles at Wimbledon between 1948 and 1955.**

9. **March 12 1914: This Welsh boxer was the first man to challenge Joe Louis for the world heavyweight title.**

10. **March 14 1936: This golfer was the first left handed player to win the British Open championship.**

ANSWERS

STAR BIRTHDATES, Capricorn (Page 69): 1. Colin Cowdrey; 2. John
Charles; 3. Frank McLintock; 4. Jess Willard; 5. Gordon Banks; 6. Rocky
Graziano; 7. Floyd Patterson; 8. Barry John; 9. Christine
Truman; 10. Muhammad Ali.

Your
Score

Running
Total

STAR BIRTHDATES — Aries

1. **March 26 1916:** This family cricketer scored 13 centuries in the 'golden' summer of 1947.

2. **March 29 1934:** This manager guided John Stracey, Maurice Hope, Jim Watt and Charlie Magri to world titles.

3. **March 31 1878:** This world boxing champion won the world heavyweight title in Sydney, Australia.

4. **April 2 1926:** This Hungarian-born footballer was famed and feared for his left foot shooting with Real Madrid.

5. **April 5 1922:** This multi-talented footballer was the pride of Preston and was always bracketed with Matthews.

6. **April 9 1957:** This exciting golfer was British Open champion in 1979 and again in 1984.

7. **April 10 1929:** This motor racing ace became the first British driver to win the world championship in 1958.

8. **April 12 1941:** This footballer climbed the Wembley steps as a winning captain in 1964, 1965 and, best of all, 1966.

9. **April 14 1923:** This Argentinian golfer beat Jack Nicklaus by two shots to win the 1967 British Open.

10. **April 15 1901:** This snooker player was world champion for 20 years and made the first maximum 147 break.

ANSWERS

Your Score | Running Total

STAR BIRTHDATES, Aquarius (Page 70): 1. Jack Nicklaus; 2. Bob Paisley; 3. Jersey Joe Walcott; 4. Stanley Matthews; 5. Dino Zoff; 6. Fred Trueman; 7. Mary Rand (Toomey); 8. John Surtees; 9. Kevin Keegan;10. John McEnroe.

STAR BIRTHDATES Taurus

1. **April 25 1947: This footballer starred with Ajax and Barcelona and was three times European player of the year.**

2. **April 26 1918: This first lady of the track won four gold medals in the 1948 Olympics in London.**

3. **April 28 1942: This cricketer skippered Middlesex and England and was a prolific run scorer for Cambridge.**

4. **April 29 1947: This American golfer won the British Open in 1976 with a last round 66 at Royal Birkdale.**

5. **May 3 1920: This boxer won the world middleweight title five times during a remarkable 201-fight career.**

6. **May 5 1945: This footballer was a Blackpool player when he won a World Cup winners' medal with England.**

7. **May 7 1914: This Australian jockey won the 1964 Epsom Derby on Santa Claus.**

8. **May 8 1932: This boxer twice knocked out Floyd Patterson in one round in world title fights.**

9. **May 13 1914: This boxer made a record 25 successful defences of the world heavyweight championship.**

10. **May 18 1909: This British tennis player completed a hat-trick of victories at Wimbledon.**

ANSWERS

STAR BIRTHDATES, Pisces (Page 71): 1. Ron Clarke; 2. Niki Lauda; 3. Denis Law; 4. Terry Spinks; 5. David Broome; 6. Kenny Dalglish; 7. Vivian Richards; 8. Louise Brough; 9. Tommy Farr; 10. Bob Charles.

Your Score

Running Total

STAR BIRTHDATES   Gemini

1. May 22 1918: This all-rounder played for Middlesex and Arsenal and scored 17 centuries in the summer of '47.

2. May 25 1898: This boxer took the world heavyweight title from Jack Dempsey and retired as undefeated champ.

3. May 26 1909: This manager hit a memorable peak when he guided Manchester United to the European Cup.

4. May 27 1912: This American golfing master was the first post-war British Open winner.

5. May 31 1929: This elegant batman captained Surrey and England and heads the Test selectors.

6. May 23 1863: This freckle-faced boxer knocked out James J. Corbett to become world champion.

7. June 6 1956: This tennis player won five successive championships on the Wimbledon Centre Court.

8. June 7 1928: This British boxer held the world middle-weight title for 64 days in 1951.

9. June 12 1945: This goalkeeper won a world record 119 caps over a span of 23 seasons.

10. June 20 1903: This batsman captained England in the immediate post-war years and played for Gloucestershire.

Your Score   Running Total

ANSWERS

1. **June 23 1916:** This Yorkshire opener was the first regular professional captain of England in Test cricket.

2. **June 24 1895:** This boxer drew the first million-dollar gate when he fought Georges Carpentier.

3. **June 26 1919:** This British boxer lost his world light-heavyweight title to Joey Maxim in 1950.

4. **July 1 1961:** This athlete emulated Jesse Owens by winning four gold medals in the Los Angeles Olympics.

5. **July 4 1926:** This Argentinian-born footballer scored a hat-trick for Real Madrid in the 1960 European Cup Final.

6. **July 5 1929:** This left-arm spin bowler played for Surrey, Leicestershire and Western Australia.

7. **July 10 1945:** This tennis player beat Betty Stove to win the women's title in the Wimbledon centenary year.

8. **July 12 1947:** This Rugby player had winning partnerships with Barry John and Phil Bennett.

9. **July 18 1949:** This bowler held the world record for most Test wickets until overtaken by Ian Botham.

10. **July 19 1946:** This excitable tennis player was a losing Wimbledon finalist against Stan Smith and Bjorn Borg.

ANSWERS

STAR BIRTHDATES, Taurus (Page 73): 1. Johan Cruyff; 2. Fanny Blankers-Koen; 3. Mike Brearley; 4. Johnny Miller; 5. Sugar Ray Robinson; 6. Alan Ball; 7. Scobie Breasley; 8. Sonny Liston; 9. Joe Louis; 10. Fred Perry.

Your Score

Running Total

STAR BIRTHDATES   Leo

1. July 31 1951: This tennis player won her first Wimbledon title in 1971 and her second when a mum nine years later.

2. August 1 1924: This West Indian captain scored 3860 Test runs between 1947 and 1963 and was knighted.

3. August 4 1958: This runner has set more then 20 world records but tripped up in the Los Angeles Olympics.

4. August 5 1948: This goalkeeper started his career with Scunthorpe and has played more than 1,000 matches.

5. August 13 1912: This golfer won the British Open in 1953 after surviving an horrific car crash.

6. August 16 1912: This footballer played for Arsenal and England and managed 1955 champions Chelsea.

7. August 17 1951: This boxer was world middleweight champion until defending against Marvin Hagler.

8. August 18 1920: This Kent and England wicket-keeper held 173 catches in 91 Tests.

9. August 22 1957: This snooker player won the world title for the first time in 1981 when he beat Doug Mountjoy.

10. August 23 1929: This Australian golfer won five British Open championships between 1954 and 1965.

Your Score   *Running Total*

ANSWERS

STAR BIRTHDATES, Gemini (Page 74): 1. Denis Compton; 2. Gene Tunney; 3. Matt Busby; 4. Sam Snead; 5. Peter May; 6. Bob Fitzsimmons; 7. Bjorn Borg; 8. Randolph Turpin; 9. Pat Jennings; 10. Walter Hammond.

STAR BIRTHDATES   Virgo

1. **August 25 1927:** This tennis player was the first black champion at Wimbledon.

2. **August 27 1908:** This batsman retired in 1948 with an incredible Test match average of 99.94.

3. **August 29 1947:** This motor racing driver beat Niki Lauda by one point to win the world championship in 1976.

4. **August 31 1944:** This cricketer played for Lancashire and was the most successful of all West Indian captains.

5. **September 1 1923:** This boxer won all his 49 fights and took the world heavyweight title from Jersey Joe Walcott.

6. **September 2 1952:** This tennis player beat Ken Rosewall and John McEnroe in Wimbledon finals.

7. **September 4 1949:** This golfer won his fifth British Open title at Royal Birkdale in 1983.

8. **September 9 1949:** This skater was the men's figure skating champion at the 1976 Olympics.

9. **September 10 1929:** This golfer won two successive British Open titles in 1961 and 1962.

10. **September 12 1913:** This all-round athlete won four gold medals in the 1936 Berlin Olympics.

ANSWERS

STAR BIRTHDATES, Cancer (Page 75): 1. Len Hutton; 2. Jack Dempsey; 3. Freddie Mills; 4. Carl Lewis; 5. Alfredo di Stefano; 6. Tony Lock; 7. Virginia Wade; 8. Gareth Edwards; 9. Dennis Lillee; 10. Ilie Nastase.

Your Score

Running Total

STAR BIRTHDATES　Libra

1. September 26 1943: This cricketer was followed by his younger brother as captain of Australia.

2. September 28 1905: This boxer became world champion on a foul and was first to beat Joe Louis

3. October 3 1921: This bowler usually shared the new ball in Test matches with Keith Miller.

4. October 6 1919: This head man of football played for Everton, Notts County, Chelsea, Brentford and Arsenal.

5. October 8 1932: This snooker player has won seven world titles and is nicknamed 'Dracula.'

6. October 9 1955: This athlete won the 800 metres in the 1980 Olympics in Moscow.

7. October 11 1937: This footballer won a World Cup medal in 1966 and captained the 1968 European Cup winners.

8. October 14 1960: This athlete lowered the world mile record to 3min. 46.32sec. in 1985.

9. October 21 1940: This batsman completed his century of centuries in a Test match at Headingley.

10. October 23 1940: This footballer played for Santos and New York Cosmos and scored more than 1,000 goals.

Your Score

Running Total

ANSWERS

STAR BIRTHDATES   Scorpio

1. October 26 1906: This boxer took the world heavy-weight title from Jack Sharkey and lost it to Max Baer.

2. October 27 1957: This footballer wore the No 10 shirt for the 1982 FA Cup winners.

3. October 30 1941: This English-born goalkeeper was the last line of defence for Arsenal and played for Scotland.

4. November 1 1935: This golfer has won 3 British Opens and was the first overseas US Open winner for 45 years.

5. November 2 1934: This great Australian tennis player was a runner-up in four Wimbledon singles finals.

6. November 3 1945: This footballer was nicknamed 'Der Bomber' and set a World Cup scoring record with 14 goals.

7. November 5 1935: This jockey rode his first St Leger victory on St Paddy in 1960.

8. November 14 1904: This Notts fast bowler spearheaded England's attack in the 'Bodyline' Test series.

9. November 16: This boxer knocked out Gerrie Coetzee in one round in a world heavyweight title eliminator.

10. November 22 1967: This tennis player became the youngest men's Wimbledon champion at 17.

ANSWERS

STAR BIRTHDATES, Virgo (Page 77): 1. Althea Gibson; 2. Donald Bradman; 3. James Hunt; 4. Clive Lloyd; 5. Rocky Marciano; 6. Jimmy Connors; 7. Tom Watson; 8. John Curry; 9. Arnold Palmer; 10. Jesse Owens.

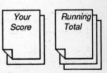

Your Score   Running Total

1. **November 23 1934:** This Australian tennis player was men's Wimbledon champion in 1956 and 1957.

2. **November 24 1955:** This cricketing all-rounder scored a memorable 149 not out at Headingley in 1981.

3. **December 1 1939:** This golfer was British Open champion in 1971 and retained the title the following year.

4. **December 3 1923:** This Essex and England all-rounder was nicknamed 'Barnacle.'

5. **December 6 1905:** This boxer took the world title from Max Baer and was called the Cinderella Man.

6. **December 8 1941:** This footballer is the only player ever to score a hat-trick in a World Cup Final.

7. **December 13 1952:** This National Hunt jockey rode a record 1138 winners.

8. **December 16 1882:** This batsman opened for Surrey and England and scored a record 197 centuries.

9. **December 17 1934:** This footballer wore the No 3 shirt in England's 1966 World Cup-winning team.

10. **December 21 1954:** This tennis player won the first of her Wimbledon titles when beating Olga Morozova in 1974.

Your Score   Running Total

ANSWERS

STAR BIRTHDATES, Libra (Page 78): 1. Ian Chappell; 2. Max Schmeling; 3. Ray Lindwall; 4.Tommy Lawton; 5. Ray Reardon; 6. Steve Ovett; 7. Bobby Charlton; 8. Steve Cram; 9. Geoff Boycott; 10. Pele.

48 ON THE BALL

Just answer 'yes' or 'no' to these football questions. One point for each correct answer and a bonus of one each time you get three right in succession.
Average score: 11 Greavsie:14

1. Did Bobby Robson play League football for West Brom?
YES/NO

2. Was Clive Allen ever on Orient's books?
YES/NO

3. Can you score direct from a corner-kick?
YES/NO

4. Has Peter Shilton won more England caps than Gordon Banks?
YES/NO

5. Do Hearts play their home games at Easter Road Park?
YES/NO

6. Is David O'Leary a Londoner by birth?
YES/NO

7. Did Mike England start his playing career with Blackburn?
YES/NO

8. Were the 1962 World Cup finals staged in Chile?
YES/NO

9. Do Norwich City play their home games at Canary Road?
YES/NO

10. Did Stanley Matthews ever score a goal in an FA Cup Final?
YES/NO

11. Have Aston Villa had a home ground other than Villa Park?
YES/NO

12. Was Bob Stokoe capped during his playing career?
YES/NO

13. Did Neville Southall ever play for Port Vale?
YES/NO

14. Has Gordon Strachan won more caps than Martin Buchan?
YES/NO

15. Did Martin Peters win an FA Cup winners' medal?
YES/NO

ANSWERS

STAR BIRTHDATES, Scorpio (Page 79): 1. Primo Carnera; 2. Glenn Hoddle; 3. Bob Wilson; 4. Gary Player; 5. Ken Rosewall; 6. Gerd Muller; 7. Lester Piggott; 8. Harold Larwood; 9. Frank Bruno; 10. Boris Becker.

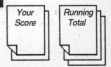

Your Score | Running Total

ALL ★ AMERICAN

There are 7 questions here about the American sports scene. A point for each correct answer.

Average score: 3   Greavsie: 4

1. In which sport was 'Yogi' Berra a household hero in the United States?

a) Basketball; b) American Football; c) Baseball

2. Which American boxing idol changed his name from Walker Smith?

a) Joe Louis; b) Ray Robinson; c) Ezzard Charles

3. How many golf courses are there in the United States?

a) 5,000-6,000 ; b) 8,000-10,000; c) 12,000-14,000

4. Which jockey has ridden more than 8,500 winners on US tracks since 1949?

a) Willie Shoemaker; b) Chris McCarron; c) Laffitt Pincay

5. In the Super Bowl, which gridiron team had a record four victories between 1975 and 1980?

a) Washington Redskins; b) LA Raiders; c) Pittsburgh Steelers

6. Which team has had most victories in the baseball World Series?

a) L.A. Dodgers; b) Chicago White Sox; c) N.Y. Yankees

7. In which city is the Astrodome where many major sporting events are promoted?

a) St. Louis; b) Houston; c) San Francisco

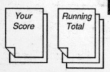

Your Score   Running Total

ANSWERS

STAR BIRTHDATES, Sagittarius (Page 80): 1 Lew Hoad; 2. Ian Botham; 3. Lee Trevino; 4. Trevor Bailey; 5. James J. Braddock; 6. Geoff Hurst; 7. John Francome; 8. Jack Hobbs; 9. Ray Wilson; 10. Chris Evert.

50
WHAT'S HIS NAME...?

There are 20 sports stars on this page labelled only by their nickname. Award yourself one point for each correct identification.
Average score: 12
Greavsie: 15

1. Fighting Marine (Boxing)

2. Clown Prince (Football)

3. The Bouncing Basque (Lawn Tennis)

4. Stork In Shorts (Athletics) **5.** The Typhoon (Cricket)

6. Whirlwind (Snooker) **7.** Gorgeous Gussie (Tennis)

8. Sniffer (Football) **9.** Old Stoneface (Boxing)

10. The Kid (horse racing) **11.** The Boot (Rugby)

12. White Lightning (Athletics) **13.** Supermex (Golf)

14. Deadly (Cricket) **15.** Merve the Swerve (Rugby)

16. The Jarrow Arrow (Athletics) **17.** Big Cat (Cricket)

18. The Whitechapel Whirlwind (Boxing)

19. Crazy Horse (Football) **20.** Kipper (Cricket)

ANSWERS

ON THE BALL (Page 81): 1. Yes; 2. No; 3. Yes; 4. Yes; 5. No (Hibs play at Easter Road; Hearts at Tynecastle Park); 6. Yes; 7. Yes; 8. Yes; 9. No (Carrow Road); 10. No; 11. Yes (Aston Park and Perry Barr); 12. No; 13. Yes (on loan); 14. Yes; 15 No.

Your Score

Running Total

*Here are four sporting mysteries for
you to solve. Award yourself two points
for each correct answer.*
Average score: 2   Greavsie: 4

1. It's a well known fact that Garfield Sobers scored a world
record six successive sixes off the bowling of Malcolm Nash at
Swansea in 1968. What is not so well known is that there was a
four minute delay between the fifth and sixth balls. **What
caused the hold-up?**

2. Joe Mercer collected the FA Cup from the Queen (now the
Queen Mother) after leading Arsenal to victory over Liverpool at
Wembley in 1950. Joe was just about to take the Cup down the
steps when he was told to go back. The mystery is: **Why was
skipper Mercer recalled?**

3. Alan Shepherd is not a name that comes instantly to mind
when you are thinking of great golfers, yet he once had a shot
that was watched by the biggest of all television audiences. **Why
did his golf shot attract such interest?**

4. Richard Raskind was beaten in straight sets by Neale Fraser
at Wimbledon in 1960. Seventeen years later the same player was
again beaten in straight sets at Wimbledon. **What was so
unique about the second match?**

ANSWERS

ALL AMERICAN (Page 82): 1 Baseball; 2 Ray Robinson; 3 12,500; 4
Willie Shoemaker; 5 Pittsburgh Steelers; 6 New York Yankees; 7
Houston.

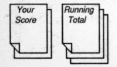

Your
Score

Running
Total

52
HARK WHO'S TALKING

There are quotes on this page from five famous sports personalities. Award yourself one point for each that you correctly identify.
Average score: 2
Greavsie: 4

1. "I saw that Tilkowski was off his line and decided to take a shot at goal. As the ball flew into the net I was aware that people were on the pitch and I didn't know whether the goal stood or not."
a) Geoff Hurst; b) Bobby Charlton; c) Roger Hunt

2. "As soon as I landed with the left I knew that was it. Berbick was not going to recover. I was throwing hydrogen bombs out there."
a) Larry Holmes; b) Tim Witherspoon; c) Mike Tyson

3. "Ian's incredible knock gave the whole team a lift. It was like coming back from the dead. I just went out there determined to bowl flat out and everything went just right for me. The Aussies still can't believe it."
a) Graham Dilley; b) Bob Willis; c) John Lever

4. "I suddenly got superstitious and put on my lucky shoes for the final session. It seemed to work. When I won the title at 18-12 I had the satisfaction of knowing I had beaten the greatest player in the world."
a) Dennis Taylor; b) Joe Johnson; c) Terry Griffiths

5. "I weigh not much more than when I started my career, but I'm retiring with a wallet that's a little heavier than it used to be."
a) Ken Rosewall; b) Charlie Magri; c) John Francome

ANSWERS

Your Score

Running Total

Do you know your way around the sports world? This will test you. One point each time you know where you are. **Average score: 6 Greavsie: 9**

53 GOING PLACES

Where are you when you're watching...

1. League football at Home Park

2. Test cricket at Eden Gardens

3. The Grand National

4. A motor racing Grand Prix at Watkins Glen

5. World championship boxing at King's Hall

6. The US Open golf championship at Winged Foot

7. Lawn Tennis at the Kooyong Stadium

8. The Prix de l'Arc de Triomphe

9. A Rugby Union international at Arms Park

10. International athletics at the Bislett stadium

11. Tobogganing on the Cresta Run

12. International football at the Nep-Stadion

ANSWERS

Your Score

Running Total

SPORTING MYSTERIES (Page 84): The umpires were debating whether Sobers had been caught but ruled that the fielder fell over the boundary when taking the catch; 2. King George V1 spotted that Mercer had been given a losers' medal by mistake. 3. It was struck on the moon with a 6-iron by the Apollo 14 astronaut in 1971. 4.It was against Virginia Wade and Richard had become Renee Richards following a sex-change operation.

54 *TEE TIME*

You score a point for each correct answer to these golfing questions.

Average score: 3 Greavsie: 4

1. On which course did Tom Watson beat Jack Nicklaus by one stroke to win the British Open in 1977?
a) Turnberry; b) Royal Lytham; c) Royal Troon

2. Which great golfer was nicknamed The Maestro?
a) Bobby Jones; b) Gene Sarazen; c) Henry Cotton

3. Who made up a seven stroke deficit to win the US Open championship for the only time in 1960?
a) Doug Sanders; b) Julius Boros; c) Arnold Palmer

4. How many times did Harry Vardon win the British Open title?
a) Six; b) Seven; c) Eight

5. The record lowest round of 63 in the US Masters was set in 1986 by which golfer?
a) Nick Price; b) Sandy Lyle; c) Bob Tway

6. Which golfer has made a record ten appearances in the Walker Cup?
a) Michael Bonallack; b) Joe Carr; c) Roger Wethered

7. Who holds the record for winning 20 Ryder Cup matches?
a) Billy Casper; b) Jack Nicklaus; c) Gene Littler

8. In 1977, who became the first non-Asian winner of the Japanese Open?
a) Nick Faldo; b) Greg Norman; c) Severiano Ballesteros

ANSWERS

HARK WHO'S TALKING (Page 85): 1 Geoff Hurst (after his third goal in the 1966 World Cup Final); 2 Mike Tyson (after winning the world title); 3 Bob Willis (after taking 8-43 against Australia at Headingley in 1981); 4 Joe Johnson (after winning the world title in 1986); 5 Ken Rosewall (talking about his retirement from tournament tennis).

Your Score

Running Total

55 ANYONE FOR TENNIS?

There are three sets of six questions on tennis here. Award yourself one point for each correct answer and a bonus of five points if you get at least four right in each set. **Average score: 8 Greavsie: 10**

FIRST SET

1. Who was the first post-war men's Wimbledon champion?
a) Jack Kramer; b) Yvon Petra;
c) Bob Falkenberg
2. Which player has appeared in most Davis Cup rubbers?
a) Nicola Pietrangeli; b) Neale Fraser; c) Henri Cochet
3. In which year did Rod Laver complete his first Grand Slam?
a) 1962; b) 1966; c) 1969
4. How many Wimbledon titles did Billie-Jean King win?
a) 16; b) 18; c) 20
5. Which of these women was a world class table tennis player?
a) Ann Jones; b) Shirley Fry;
c) Alice Marble
6. In which year did Fred Perry last win at Wimbledon?
a) 1938; b) 1937; c) 1936

SECOND SET

1. Who played in a record 55 rubbers in the Wightman Cup?
a) Christine Truman; b) Virginia Wade; c) Angela Mortimer
2. Tom Okker was a top-class player in which other sport?
a) Boxing; b) Hockey; c) Soccer
3. In which year did Bjorn Borg win his first Wimbledon title?
a) 1976; b) 1977; c) 1978
4. How many times was Ken Rosewall Wimbledon runner-up?
a) Three; b) Four; c) Five
5. Which tennis star was the son of a Scottish pro. footballer?
a) Donald Budge; b) Tony Trabert; c) Chuck McKinley
6. Which great champion was nicknamed 'Miss Poker Face'?
a) Louise Brough; b) Helen Wills-Moody; c) Maria Bueno

THIRD SET

1. Who was the first player to win three men's US Opens?
a) John McEnroe; b) Jimmy Connors; c) Bjorn Borg
2. Margaret Court was talented at which other sport?
a) Golf; b) Squash; c) Netball
3. In which year was the tie-break introduced at Wimbledon?
a) 1971; b) 1973; c) 1975

4. How many times was John Newcombe Wimbledon champion?
a) Three; b) Four; c) Five
5. Who did Pancho Gonzales beat in a 112-game Wimbledon match?
a) Budge Patty; b) Fred Stolle;
c) Charlie Pasarell
6. Who has a tennis ranch in Spain?
a) Roger Taylor; b) Lew Hoad;
c) Vic Seixas

ANSWERS

Your Score

Running Total

56 SEARCH FOR A STAR

How many modern international footballers can you find in this grid? There are 20 surnames. Some appear in straight-forward, left-to-right formations, others are printed in reverse or diagonally across the page. Award yourself one point for each name that you find. **Average score: 12   Greavsie: 15**

P	H	O	D	G	E	N	O	T	L	I	H	S
I	L	U	Z	A	R	D	I	L	E	S	L	N
H	B	D	A	L	G	L	I	S	H	A	A	J
L	O	E	S	T	R	E	B	O	R	L	W	N
L	B	D	L	R	O	B	S	O	N	D	R	A
A	E	H	D	O	Q	U	I	N	N	R	E	H
H	A	S	V	L	K	A	Z	M	S	I	N	C
T	R	P	X	C	E	Y	L	H	R	D	S	A
U	D	E	W	A	R	K	V	L	F	G	O	R
O	S	E	P	S	D	O	O	W	E	N	T
S	L	D	B	R	A	D	Y	P	M	N	B	S
Q	E	I	E	D	I	S	E	T	I	H	W	G
K	Y	E	S	A	L	O	H	C	I	N	J	U

ANSWERS

TEE TIME (Page 87): 1.Turnberry; 2. Henry Cotton; 3. Arnold Palmer; 4. Six times; 5. Nick Price; 6. Joe Carr; 7. Billy Casper; 8. Severiano Ballesteros.

Your Score

Running Total

89

57 THE FIVE STAR TEST

Award yourself one point for each correct identification in this five-star test.

Average score: 14 Greavsie: 19

1. Which five of these athletes won Olympic gold medals: Chris Brasher, Chris Chataway, Ronnie Delany, Derek Ibbotson, Ann Packer, Sydney Wooderson, Eric Liddell, Harold Abrahams, John Disley, David Bedford.

2. Which five of these footballers did not win FA Cup winners medals during their career: Billy Wright, Tom Finney, Tommy Lawton, Les Allen, Len Shackleton, Johnny Byrne, Gordon Banks, John Hollins, Nobby Stiles, Ray Wilson.

3. Which five of these bowlers took more than 250 Test wickets: Alec Bedser, Bob Willis, Richie Benaud, Lance Gibbs, Jim Laker, Brian Statham, John Snow, Derek Underwood, Ray Lindwall, Kapil Dev.

4. Which five of these golfers have never won the US Masters: Bobby Locke, Tom Weiskopf, Craig Stadler, Ray Floyd, Billy Casper, Byron Nelson, Hale Irwin, Johnny Miller, Lee Trevino, Fuzzy Zoeller.

5. Which five of these boxers fought Sugar Ray Robinson more than once in world title fights: Kid Gavilan, Rocky Graziano, Gene Fullmer, Joey Maxim, Randolph Turpin, Carmen Basilio, Jake LaMotta, Paul Pender, Carlo Olson, Joey Giardello.

Your Score	Running Total

ANSWERS

ANYONE FOR TENNIS? (Page 88): Set 1 - 1. Yvon Petra; 2. Nicola Pietrangeli; 3. 1962; 4. 20; 5. Ann Jones; 6. 1936; Set 2 - 1. Virginia Wade; 2. Soccer; 3. 1976; 4. Four; 5. Donald Budge; 6. Helen Wills-Moody; Set 3 - 1. Jimmy Connors; 2. Squash; 3. 1971; 4. Three; 5. Charlie Pasarell; 6. Lew Hoad.

58 FIRST PAST THE POST

The questions on this page all relate to the Grand National. One point for each correct answer. **Average score: 5 Greavsie: 6**

1. On which horse did Fred Winter ride his first National winner at Aintree in 1957?
   a) Sundew; b) Kilmore; c) Jay Trump

2. Which jockey had his only National victory on Anglo in 1966?
   a) Graham Thorner; b) Tim Norman; c) Dave Dick

3. Which trainer saddled 1981 winner Aldaniti?
   a) Guy Balding; b) Josh Gifford; c) Tim Forster

4. Specify was a winner for which owner in 1971?
   a) Paul Raymond; b) Raymond Guest; c) Fred Pontin

5. Which was the first post-war 100-1 winner?
   a) Caughoo; b) Ayala; c) Foinavon

6. In which year did Pat Taaffe win on Gay Trip?
   a) 1965; b) 1970; c) 1975

7. Which horse overtook Devon Loch to win in 1956?
   a) Quare Times; b) Oxo; c) E.S.B.

8. Who was the first woman rider to complete the Grand National course at Aintree?
   a) Charlotte Brew; b) Geraldine Rees; c) Elaine Mellor

ANSWERS

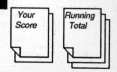

Your Score | Running Total

Imagine you are a batsman facing a 6-ball over. But against who? Award yourself a point for each bowler you identify from the clues.
Average score: 3 Greavsie: 4

1. This fast bowler was born in Jamaica in 1954 and has represented Derbyshire in County cricket. He took 14 England wickets for 149 runs in the 1976 Oval Test.

2. Now you are facing the pace of an English bowler who during an 18-year career took 2,260 wickets, including 252 in Tests. He captained Lancashire for two seasons.

3. Our third paceman is an Australian whose left arm quickies brought him 186 wickets in 44 Tests between 1952 and 1963. He was also a good-class bat.

4. A master of seam bowling is next to put you to the Test. He took 236 wickets in 51 Tests for England and was the heart of the Surrey attack across two decades. Now a respected cricket administrator.

5. This West Indian spinner played for Guyana and Warwickshire and he once held the world Test record with 309 wickets. He was also a specialist fielder who held 203 Test catches.

6. Finally, we have a masterly Indian slow left-arm bowler who was easily recognisable because of his colourful turbans. In 67 Tests for India, he took 266 wickets. He was a particular favourite at Northants.

ANSWERS

Your Score

Running Total

Can you fill in the blanks in the following sporting headlines? Award yourself one point for each gap that you fill.
Average score: 7
Greavsie: 11

1.
BLANK STOPS PATTERSON IN THIRD ROUND TO WIN TITLE

2.
EDDERY RIDES BLANK TO HIS FIRST DERBY VICTORY

3.
BLANK'S SUPER SHOT CLINCHES DOUBLE FOR MEE'S MARVELS

4.
BLANK BEATS RODGERS IN PLAY-OFF FOR THE 1963 OPEN TITLE

5.
BLANK PIPS AOUITA AND SETS NEW WORLD RECORD

6.
SKIPPER BLANK NETS GOAL NUMBER FOUR FOR BRAZIL AS THEY OUTPLAY ITALY IN 1970 WORLD CUP FINAL

7.
'LAST TEST' BRADMAN BOWLED FOR A DUCK BY BLANK

8.
BLANK KICKS 22 GOALS IN ONE RUGBY LEAGUE GAME

9.
BLANK CONQUERS BILLIE-JEAN ON HER WAY TO COMPLETING 1970 GRAND SLAM

10.
'THE BELL WENT DING AND I WENT DONG' SAYS WORLD CHAMPION BLANK

11.
'KEEPER BLANK CLAIMS RECORD 10TH VICTIM IN 1980 BOMBAY TEST

14.
BLANK BEAT CREWE 13-2 IN CUP REPLAY

12.
BLANK FIRST TO BEAT HOLMES

13.
BLANK WINS 400 METRES HURDLES IN '68 GAMES

ANSWERS

FIRST PAST THE POST (Page 91): 1 Sundew; 2 Tim Norman; 3 Josh Gifford; 4 Fred Pontin; 5 Caughoo; 6 1970; 7 E.S.B.; 8 Geraldine Rees (who finished last on Cheers in the 1982 Grand National).

Your Score

Running Total

61

SECONDS OUT!

You have got to go 10 rounds with 10 different world boxing champions from the past. Award yourself one point each time you can identify your opponent. Give yourself a five point knockout bonus if you can name 7 or more.
Average score: 5   Greavsie: 6

Round 1: This Argentinian was Olympic flyweight champion in 1948 and world flyweight king for six years from 1954.

Round 2: An Australian Aboriginal, this bantamweight successfully defended his world title against Britain's Alan Rudkin.

Round 3: Your featherweight opponent is a Welshman who had three memorable battles with Vicente Saldivar.

Round 4: Now you're in against a great lightweight champion who twice beat Britain's Dave Charnley for the world crown.

Round 5: Coming out from the light-welterweight corner is the pre-war East End idol who was dubbed the Whitechapel Whirlwind.

Round 6: This fighter was welter and middleweight champion and numbered Brian Curvis and Dave Charnley among his victims.

Round 7: Your light-middleweight opponent was a 1960 Olympic champion and one of Italy's greatest ring heroes.

Round 8: The one and only 'Paddington Express' comes steaming out of his corner to fight for the middleweights.

Round 9: This light-heavyweight champion was an 'ageless' wonder who defended his title against Yolande Pompey in 1956.

Round 10: Finally, you are matched against the former world heavyweight champion who was known as the 'Black Uhlan'.

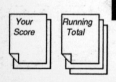

Your Score

Running Total

ANSWERS

HOWZAT (Page 92): 1. Michael Holding; 2. Brian Statham; 3. Alan Davidson; 4. Alec Beder; 5. Lance Gibbs; 6. Bishen Bedi.

*See how quickly you can identify
a star sportsman from the clues.*
Average score: 4   Greavsie: 6

For 12 points: Our mystery guest was born in Glasgow in 1948 and took up his sport in the winter of 1963 after heavy snow had prevented him playing football.

For 10 points: He was selected for the 1968 Olympics but declined to take part because he did not think he had sufficient experience.

For 8 points: He knocked out John Stracey in one round in the 1968 ABA championships before turning professional as a lightweight.

For 6 points: It was after joining the Terry Lawless stable that he became a major star, and he won the European lightweight title by stoping Andre Holyk in one round in Glasgow.

For 4 points: A southpaw, he became the world lightweight champion by stopping Alfredo Pitalua in 12 rounds at Kelvin Hall in 1979.

For 2 points: He made four successful defences of the world crown before losing on points to Alexis Arguello at Wembley in 1981. Now a successful businessman, he is the regular ringside summariser for ITV alongside commentator Reg Gutteridge.

ANSWERS

HEADLINE MAKERS (Page 93: 1. Ingemar Johansson; 2. Grundy; 3. Charlie George; 4. Bob Charles; 5. Steve Cram; 6. Carlos Alberto; 7. Eric Hollies; 8. Jim Sullivan; 9. Margaret Court; 10. Lloyd Honeyghan; 11. Bob Taylor; 12. Michael Spinks; 13. David Hemery; 14. Tottenham.

Your Score

Running Total

You have five minutes to answer each teaser. You get one point for each correct answer and a 5-point bonus each time you beat the clock.

63 BEAT THE CLOCK

Average score: 32 Greavsie: 42

1. Name the nine clubs that won the FA Cup during the 1970s.

2. Name the six Derby winners trained by Vincent O'Brien.

3. Name the eight British boxers who have held the world flyweight title since 1930.

4. Name the eight batsmen who had scored more than 5,000 Test runs for England before the mid-1980s.

5. Name the seven men who have managed Manchester United since the war.

Your Score

Running Total

ANSWERS

SECONDS OUT (Page 94): 1. Pascual Perez; 2. Lionel Rose; 3. Howard Winstone; 4. Joe Brown; 5. Jack (Kid) Berg; 6. Emile Griffith; 7. Nino Benvenuti; 8. Terry Downes; 9. Archie Moore; 10. Max Schmeling.

64
MORE ODD MEN OUT

Who is the odd man out in each of the following six lists? We give you a little 'think hint' to help. Award yourself one point for each correct answer.
Average score: 2 Greavsie: 5

1. Sports celebrities Harvey Smith, Brian Clough, Freddie Trueman, Brendan Foster, Bruce Woodcock, Derek Ibbotson, Geoff Boycott. *Think counties.*

2. Footballers Kevin Keegan, Trevor Brooking, Alan Taylor, Ricky Villa, Malcolm Macdonald, Billy Bremner, David Webb. *Think FA Cup Final goals.*

3. World champion boxers Floyd Patterson, Muhammad Ali, Joe Frazier, George Foreman, Larry Holmes, Leon Spinks, Michael Spinks. *Think Olympics.*

4. Test cricketers Garfield Sobers, Neil Harvey, John Edrich, David Gower, Dennis Amiss, Clive Lloyd, Graeme Pollock. *Think left.*

5. Tennis players Jaroslav Drobny, Jimmy Connors, John McEnroe, Budge Patty, Pancho Gonzales, Dick Savitt, Ashley Cooper. *Think Wimbledon.*

6. Rugby internationals Serge Blanco, JPR Williams, Dusty Hare, John Rutherford, Don Clarke, Tom Kiernan, Bob Hiller. *Think back!*

ANSWERS

GUESS THE GUEST (Page 95): The mystery personality is former world lightweight boxing champion Jim Watt, who is now a popular man at the microphone for ITV.

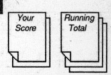

Your Score   Running Total

65 THE TRIVIA TEST

See if you can select the right answer to each of these trivial sports questions. Award yourself one point for each correct answer.
Average score: 2   Greavsie: 3

1. Which former Prime Minister was President of the MCC?
a) Edward Heath; b) Alec Douglas Home; c) Anthony Eden

2. Which football manager was once a nightclub singer?
a) Terry Venables; b) George Graham; c) Graham Taylor

3. Which world boxing champion used to have his wedding ring tied to his boxing boot?
a) Carlos Monzon; b) Willie Pastrano; c) Jose Napoles

4. Which cricketer officially adopted the name of Bob Dylan?
a) Bob Taylor; b) Bob Barber; c) Bob Willis

5. Which dog sniffed out the World Cup trophy after it had been stolen in London in 1966?
a) Patch; b) Pickles; c) Pepper

6. Which world heavyweight boxing champion had 23 brothers and sisters?
a) Sonny Liston; b) Jersey Joe Walcott; c) Floyd Patterson

7. Which one of these sportsmen once stood as a Tory candidate in an election?
a) Richard Meade; b) Jonah Barrington; c) Ted Dexter

ANSWERS

BEAT THE CLOCK (Page 96): 1. Chelsea (1970), Arsenal (1971/1979), Leeds United (1972), Sunderland (1973), Liverpool (1974), West Ham (1975), Southampton (1976), Man United (1977), Ipswich (1978). 2. Larkspur (1961), Sir Ivor (1968), Nijinsky (1970), Roberto (1972), The Minstrel (1977), Golden Fleece (1982).

 Your Score   Running Total

3. Terry Allen, Benny Lynch, Jackie Brown, Peter Kane, Jackie Paterson, Rinty Monaghan, Walter McGowan, Charlie Magri. 4. Geoff Boycott, Colin Cowdrey, Walter Hammond, Len Hutton, Ken Barrington, Denis Compton, Jack Hobbs, John Edrich. 5. Matt Busby (who had two spells as manager but has been counted only once for this quiz answer), Wilf McGuinness, Frank O'Farrell, Tommy Docherty, Dave Sexton, Ron Atkinson, Alex Ferguson.

66 SPORTS GRAM

Rearrange the letters to identify 10 Best-of-British sports stars. We give a brief clue to help. Award yourself one point for each correct answer.
Average score: 6 Greavsie 7

1. BITES ON A CHASE
A double Olympic gold medallist

2. ONLY HOLY HANGED
A busy bee of a boxer

3. A FOND LICK
He has gone a fair way to the top

4. I'D SAVE VEST
He's at the top of the table in his sport

5. NICE SLOW RAIL
This Scot has a real will to win

6. THEY PLAN MOODS
Is he an everyday sort of hero?

7. GLADLY SKIN HEN
He manages to play football as well!

8. ALL SINGLE MEN
He's a big wheel in motor sport

9. VIEW A RING AID
She often courted triumph

10. AN EVIL CELL
Goals are his spur

ANSWERS

MORE ODD MEN OUT (Page 97): 1. Brendan Foster (not a Yorkshireman); 2. Malcolm Macdonald (did not score an FA Cup Final goal); 3. Larry Holmes (did not win an Olympic gold medal). 4. Dennis Amiss (did not bat left-handed); 5. Pancho Gonzales (did not win a Wimbledon title); 6 John Rutherford (not a full back).

Your Score

Running Total

SNOOKER
BREAK

*There are a possible 147 points to be scored
on the following seven pages. Each question
has been given a points value according to
its degree of difficulty. This is a test for
all-rounders, not just snooker buffs. Only
the 7-point questions are on snooker. This
is your cue to start...*

Average score: 67 Greavsie: 105

ANSWERS

THE TRIVIA TEST (Page 98): 1. Alec Douglas Home; 2. Terry Venables; 3. Willie
Pastrano; 4. Bob Dylan Willis; 5. Pickles; 6. Sonny Liston; 7. Ted Dexter (who contested
the Cardiff South-East seat in a General Election and was beaten by the then Labour
Shadow Chancellor James Callaghan).

Who was England's leading goal scorer in the 1986 World Cup Finals in Mexico?

Did the 'Sultan of Snooker' Joe Davis win the world championship for the first time in 1927, 1930 or 1933?

In which city were the 1976 Olympics staged: Moscow, Montreal or Mexico City?

Which one of these players is not a left hander: Jimmy White, Tony Meo, Dean Reynolds, Kirk Stevens, Perrie Mans?

Did British speed ace Stirling Moss ever win the world motor racing championship?

Did Steve Davis beat Alex Higgins or Cliff Thorburn in the final when he won his second world title in 1983?

Who stopped Gerry Cooney in five rounds in a heavyweight fight in June, 1987?

Was it Terry Griffiths or John Spencer who won the world title at his first attempt in1979?

Who captained Liverpool when they won the FA Cup to complete the League-Cup double in 1986?

Did Dennis Taylor beat Tony Knowles or Jimmy White in the semi-finals of the 1985 world championship?

 Your Score

 Running Total

ANSWERS

The answers to these Snooker Break questions are on page 104.

(1)

Who was manager of Scotland when they qualified for the 1978 World Cup finals in Argentina?

(7)

Did Willie Thorne or Neal Foulds win his first major trophy in the 1985 Mercantile Credit Classic?

(1)

Did Roger Bannister break the four minute mile barrier for the first time at Oxford or Cambridge?

(7)

Which one of these players has never been world snooker champion: Fred Davis, Rex Williams, John Pulman, Walter Donaldson?

(1)

Against which club did Stanley Matthews win his only FA Cup winners' medal in 1953?

ANSWERS

SNOOKER BREAK (Page 101): 1: Gary Lineker was top scorer; 7: Joe Davis won the title for the first time in 1927; 1: Montreal hosted the 1976 Olympics; 7: Kirk Stevens does not play left handed; 1: Stirling Moss was never world motor racing champion.

Your Score

Running Total

Who beat Perrie Mans when he reached the 1978 world champion-ship final?

Did Bob Willis start his career with Surrey or Sussex before switching to Warwickshire?

Was it Dean Reynolds or John Parrott who turned professional after winning the inaugural Junior Pot Black tourn-ament?

Which jockey won the 1977 Oaks and St Leger on the Queen's horse Dun-fermline?

Who knocked defending champion Dennis Taylor out of the 1986 world championships?

ANSWERS

SNOOKER BREAK (Page 102): 7: Steve Davis beat Cliff Thorburn in the 1983 world championship final; 1: Michael Spinks stopped Gerry Cooney in 5 rounds; 7: Terry Griffiths won the world title at his first attempt in 1979; 1: Alan Hansen captained Liverpool in the 1986 FA Cup Final; 7: Tony Knowles.

Who scored England's second goal in the 1966 World Cup Final against West Germany at Wembley?

Was it 1977, 1979 or 1981 when the first Embassy World Championship was staged at The Crucible Theatre?

Which long jumper was first to beat the 28 and 29-foot barriers in the 1968 Olympic Games?

Which one of these players has played in a world snooker final: Cliff Wilson, Bill Werbeniuk, David Taylor, Kirk Stevens, Graham Miles?

Did Sugar Ray Leonard outpoint Marvin Hagler over 12 or 15 rounds in their 1987 world title fight showdown?

ANSWERS

SNOOKER BREAK (Page 103): 1: Ally Macleod was Scotland's 1978 World Cup manager; 7: Willie Thorne won the 1985 Mercantile Classic; 1: Bannister broke the 4-minute mile barrier at Oxford in 1954; 7: Rex Williams was world billiards champion but never won the snooker crown; 1: Bolton Wanderers.

Who was the third member of the Irish team with Alex Higgins and Eugene Hughes that won the 1985 World Cup?

Which Welsh footballing idol played for Leeds United and Juventus in the 1950s?

Was it Tony Meo or Terry Griffiths who partnered Steve Davis in winning the 1983 Hofmeister world doubles?

Who scored the winning goal in the 1985 FA Cup Final between Manchester United and Everton?

Name the first overseas player to win the popular BBCtv Pot Black tournament.

Did former heavyweight hero Henry Cooper win three or four Lonsdale Belts outright?

On which ground did Len Hutton score his 364 Test runs to create what was then a world record in 1938?

In which city were the 1952 Olympics staged: Amsterdam, Paris, Helsinki or Stockholm?

With which FA Cup winning team did Peter Simpson get a winners' medal ?

In which country did Muhammad Ali knock out George Foreman in 1974?

And your final pot-the-black question: Who did Alex Higgins beat in the world championship final in 1982.

ANSWERS

Your Score

Running Total

68 THE NAME GAME

EACH clue leads to a well-known name. Put the initials in the appropriate squares to identify a sports star: One point for each correct answer, plus a bonus of five points for completing the main name.

Average score: 8   Greavsie: 11

1	2	3	4	5	6	7	8

9	10	11	12	13	14

5 & 13	Was this Welshman in a hurry to sign for Juventus?
8 & 3	He deserted the England manager's job for a far post in the desert.
11 & 6	This bookmaker managed to make Barry McGuigan a good title bet.
14 &10	The 'Brighton Express' who broke the world one-mile record in 1981.
2 & 4	He was in charge in the 'Granite City' before moving to Old Trafford.
1 &12	The scrum-half idol who passed with honours for Wales in 53 matches.
9 & 7	He was world heavyweight king from 1962 until 1964.

Your Score   Running Total

ANSWERS

69
WHO DID WHAT?

Each answer in this test is a surname that starts with the same initial. Award yourself one point for each correct identification.
Average score: 7 Greavsie: 8

1. WHO steered Barcelona to the Spanish League title after helping Ajax win three European Cup Finals?

2. WHO did Lloyd Honeghan beat to win the world welter-weight title?

3. WHO won the British Open in 1934, 1937 and 1948?

4. WHO was the British driver who won the world motor racing championship in 1963 and 1965?

5. WHO was the American who defeated Ken Rosewall in the 1974 men's singles final at Wimbledon?

6. WHO was the crack Australian middle-distance runner who took the bronze medal in the 1964 Olympic 10,000 metres final?

7. WHO is the only Italian to have won the world heavyweight boxing title?

8. WHO rode Sea Bird II to victory in the 1965 Derby?

9. WHO scored the winning goal for Leeds United in the 1972 FA Cup Final?

10. WHO was the slip fielder who held 120 catches for England?

ANSWERS

SNOOKER BREAK (Page 107): 2: Henry Cooper won three Lonsdale Belts; 3: Hutton scored his 364 at The Oval; 4: The 1952 Olympics were held in Helsinki; 5: Peter Simpson won an FA Cup winner's medal with Arsenal in 1971; 6: Zaire (The Rumble in the Jungle); 7: Higgins beat Ray Reardon.

Your Score

Running Total

*Who is the odd man out in each
of the following six lists? We give
you a little 'think hint' to help.
Award yourself one point for
each correct answer.*
Average score: 4 Greavsie: 5

1. Golfers Tom Watson, Bill Rogers, Nick Faldo, Sandy Lyle, Raymond Floyd, Johnny Miller, Greg Norman, Lee Trevino. *Think Open.*

2. England footballers Gordon Banks, Nobby Stiles, Francis Lee, Roger Hunt, Alan Ball, Geoff Hurst, Martin Peters. *Think 1966.*

3. Snooker players Joe Johnson, Jimmy White, John Spencer, Ray Reardon, Steve Davis, Alex Higgins, Terry Griffiths. *Think world champions.*

4. Test bowlers Alan Davidson, Trevor Bailey, Tony Lock, Wasim Akram, Phil Edmonds, Derek Underwood, John Lever. *Think left!*

5. Olympic track champions John Walker, Sebastian Coe, Josef Barthel, Steve Ovett, Jack Lovelock, Herb Elliott, Kip Keino. *Think metric mile.*

6. Heavyweight boxers James Tillis, Tim Witherspoon, Leon Spinks, James Smith, Tony Tubbs, Greg Page, Mike Tyson. *Think world title.*

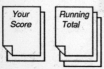

Your
Score

Running
Total

ANSWERS

THE NAME GAME (Page 108): Sir GARFIELD SOBERS (Ian Rush, Don Revie, Barney Eastwood, Steve Ovett, Alex Ferguson, Gareth Edwards, Sonny Liston).

71 THE TRIVIA TEST

See if you can select the right answer to each of these trivial sports questions. Award yourself one point for each correct answer.
Average score: 4 Greavsie: 5

1. Which England goalkeeper stretched his arms by hanging for hours on end on the bannisters at his home?
a) Ray Clemence; b) Phil Parkes; c) Peter Shilton

2. Which former world heavyweight boxing champion said 'Give me broads before boxing any day!'
a) Primo Carnera; b) Max Baer; c) Jack Johnson

3. Which top golfer once managed a topless night club band?
a) Hale Irwin; b) Ray Floyd; c) Bernhard Langer

4. Which England cricketer's mother was herself a keen all-round cricketer?
a) Ian Botham; b) Mike Gatting; c) David Gower

5. Who slept in the stable with his horse before the round in which they clinched an Olympic gold medal for Britain?
a) Harry Llewellyn; b) Richard Meade; c) David Broome

6. Whose recording of the song Head Over Heels in Love got into the Top 40?
a) Alan Birchenall; b) Terry Venables; c) Kevin Keegan

7. Which Olympic champion sculler was barred from competing at Henley because he was a bricklayer?
a) John Kelly; b) Paul Costello; c) Johannes Koen

ANSWERS

WHO DID WHAT? (Page 109): 1. Johan Cruyff; 2. Don Curry; 3. Henry Cotton; 4. Jim Clark; 5. Jimmy Connors; 6. Ron Clarke; 7. Primo Carnera; 8. Pat Glennon; 9. Allan Clarke; 10. Colin Cowdrey.

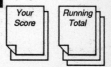
Your Score   Running Total

72 SPORTS GRAM

Rearrange the letters to identify a team of 11 England cricketers. We give a brief clue to help. Award yourself one point for each correct answer.
Average score: 7 Greavsie: 8

1. ROB SAD RICH
Man of the series down under in 1986/7.

2. NO MINOR BITS
You might expect to find him with a Swiss family!

3. GIVE DAD ROW
Left-handed artist.

4. I GET MAT KING
He bristles with runs at Lord's

5. DEER ALL DRANK
He fields at a rate of knots.

6. A BAT ON HIM
He puts plenty of beef into his performances.

7. OWN UP TO LAND
He stumped from Kent to Middlesex.

8. DIM LEND SHOP
He has batsmen in a spin.

9. STONE RIFLE
Fast man from Essex.

10. HARM LEG DAILY
He's full of bounce at Worcester.

11. GOALS MELT LANDS
You might expect him to come in at No.10.

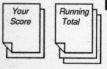

Your Score

Running Total

ANSWERS

ODD MAN OUT (page 110): 1. Raymond Floyd (has not won British Open); 2. Francis Lee (did not play in World Cup winning side); 3. Jimmy White (has not won world championship); 4. Trevor Bailey (was a right arm bowler); 5. Steve Ovett (did not win 1500 metres gold medal); 6. James Tillis (has not won world title).

73 SPORTING CINEMA

Each question relates to sports-based films. One point for each correct answer.
Average score: 3
Greavsie: 4

1. Who portrayed baseball hero Grover Cleveland in *The Winning Team?*
a) Spencer Tracy; b) Clark Gable; c) Ronald Reagan

2. In which film did Errol Flynn star as a world heavyweight boxing champion?
a) The Big Fight; b) Gentleman Jim; c) For Whom The Bell Tolls

3. Which former American football star appeared in *The Dirty Dozen?*
a) O.J. Simpson; b) Jim Brown; c) Joe Namath

4. Who played the part of a would-be champion skiier in *Downhill Racer?*
a) Robert Redford; b) Robert Vaughn; c) Robert Duvall

5. Which sport provides the background to *The Colour Of Money?*
a) Basketball; b) Pool; c) Horse Racing

6. In which film did Adam Faith play the part of a football manager?
a) Deadly Striker; b) The Second Half; c) Yesterday's Hero

7. Who plays the starring role of a boxer in *Fat City?*
a) Beau Bridges; b) Jeff Bridges; c) Lloyd Bridges

ANSWERS

THE TRIVIA TEST (Page 111): 1. Peter Shilton; 2. Max Baer; 3. Ray Floyd; 4. Ian Botham; 5. Harry Llewellyn; 6. Kevin Keegan; 7. John Kelly.

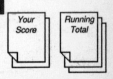

Your Score

Running Total

113

*See how quickly you can identify
a star sportsman from the clues.*
Average score: 6   Greavsie: 8

For 12 points: Our mystery guest was born in London in 1961, and made his professional debut at his sport in 1982.

For 10 points: He had to travel to Bogota to undergo an operation on his right eye before he could begin his professional career.

For 8 points: He stands 6ft 3in tall, weighs in at over 16 stone and was the youngest ever ABA heavyweight champion.

For 6 points: Under the guidance of Terry Lawless, he won his first 21 fights as a professional — all inside the distance.

For 4 points: His first defeat came in 1984 when he was knocked out in the 10th round by James 'Bone-crusher' Smith at Wembley Arena.

For 2 points: He challenged Tim Witherspoon for the world heavyweight title at Wembley Stadium in July 1986, and was giving an excellent account of himself until stopped in the 10th round.

Your Score	Running Total

ANSWERS

SPORTS GRAM (Page 112): 1. Chris Broad; 2. Tim Robinson; 3. David Gower; 4. Mike Gatting; 5. Derek Randall; 6.Ian Botham; 7. Paul Downton; 8. Phil Edmonds; 9. Neil Foster; 10. Graham Dilley; 11. Gladstone Small.

Each of the questions relate to sporting books. One point for each correct answer.
Average score: 3
Greavsie: 5

1. Who wrote the boxing novel *The Harder They Fall?*
a) Bud Schulberg; b) Norman Mailer; c) Damon Runyan

2. *Pace Like Fire* was the autobiography of which West Indian fast bowler?
a) Michael Holding; b) Charlie Griffith; c) Wes Hall

3. What was the title of the Hugh Atkinson novel based on an Olympic marathon race?
a) The Long Run; b) The Games; c) The Glory Race

4. Which former England cricket captain wrote a thriller called *Testkill?*
a) Ted Dexter; b) Freddie Brown; c) Mike Brearley

5. Who wrote the official Lester Piggott biography?
a) Brough Scott; b) Julian Wilson; c) Dick Francis

6. Which football manager had a book called *The Rat Race* cancelled before publication?
a) Lawrie McMenemy; b) Tommy Docherty; c) John Bond

7. *The Rise And Fall* told the story of which former international football star?
a) Tommy Lawton; b) George Best; c) Peter Osgood

8. Which ex-world champion wrote a book about Muhammad Ali called *Sting Like A Bee?*
a) Bob Foster; b) Archie Moore; c) Jose Torres

ANSWERS

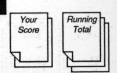

Your Score | Running Total

76

ON THE BALL

Just answer 'yes' or 'no' to these football questions. One point for each correct answer and a bonus of one each time you get three right in succession.
Average score: 9 Greavsie:12

1. Did George Graham play League football for Aston Villa?
YES/NO

2. Do Doncaster play home games at the Racecourse Ground?
YES/NO

3. Can a goal be scored direct from a goal-kick?
YES/NO

4. Did Trevor Brooking win more caps than Johnny Haynes?
YES/NO

5. Is Gordon Banks a Yorkshireman by birth?
YES/NO

6. Did Paul Walsh start his playing career with Luton Town?
YES/NO

7. Has Tommy Docherty ever managed a club in Portugal?
YES/NO

8. Were the 1958 World Cup finals staged in Sweden?
YES/NO

9. Did Jeff Astle ever score a goal in an FA Cup Final?
YES/NO

10. Has Billy Bonds ever won an England cap?
YES/NO

11. Have Aston Villa ever been in the Fourth Division?
YES/NO

12. Did Lawrie McMenemy ever play First Division football?
YES/NO

13. Were Spurs the first British team to win a European trophy?
YES/NO

14. Did Kevin Keegan net more England goals than Roger Hunt?
YES/NO

15. Has the European Cup Final ever been staged at Hampden?
YES/NO

ANSWERS

Your Score

Running Total

GUESS THE GUEST (Page 114): The mystery personality is Frank Bruno, the former European heavyweight champion.

116

77
ON A
PLATE

Here are 15 easy questions to help you boost your score. Award yourself a point for each correct answer, plus a one point bonus every time you get three successive questions right.
Average score: 11 Greavsie: 14

1. Which team is at home at Upton Park?

2. Who twice outpointed Jack Dempsey over 10 rounds?

3. With which League club did Ian Rush start his career?

4. Which West Indian made his Test debut at 17 in 1953?

5. Who was John Newcombe's regular men's doubles partner?

6. Who holds the world record in the 400 metres hurdles?

7. Bob Davies won the 1978 Grand National on which horse?

8. With which sport do you associate the name Marcus Allen?

9. Who won the British Open golf championship in 1987?

10. On which ground do Surrey play home cricket matches?

11. Who was signed by Barcelona for £2,750,000 in 1986?

12. What nationality was sprinter Don Quarrie?

13. Who won the world motor racing championship in 1984?

14. Which team beat Spurs to win the 1987 FA Cup Final?

15. Who was men's singles runner-up at Wimbledon in 1987?

ANSWERS

SPORTS BOOKSHELF (Page 115): 1. Bud Schulberg; 2. Wes Hall; 3. The Games; 4. Ted Dexter; 5. Dick Francis; 6. Tommy Docherty; 7 Tommy Lawton; 8. Jose Torres.

Your Score

Running Total

78 TEAM SHEET

There are six famous football teams below, each with a key player missing. Award yourself one point for each absentee that you spot.
Average score: 2
Greavsie: 4

1. MAN UNITED'S 1985 FA CUP WINNERS
Gary Bailey
John Gidman
Arthur Albiston
Norman Whiteside
Paul McGrath
Kevin Moran
Bryan Robson
Mark Hughes
Frank Stapleton
Jesper Olsen

2. REAL MADRID'S 1960 EUROPEAN CUP WINNERS
Dominguez
Marquitos
Pachin
Vidal
Santamaria
Zarraga
Canario
Del Sol
Di Stefano
Gento

3. LIVERPOOL'S 1977 EUROPEAN CUP WINNERS
Ray Clemence
Phil Neal
Joey Jones
Tommy Smith
Alan Kennedy
Kevin Keegan
Jimmy Case
Steve Heighway
Ian Callaghan
Terry McDermott

4. BRAZIL'S 1970 WORLD CUP WINNERS
Felix
Brito
Carlos Alberto
Piazza
Everaldo
Clodoaldo
Jairzinho
Pele
Tostao
Rivelino

5. LEEDS UNITED'S 1972 FA CUP WINNERS
Paul Reaney
Paul Madeley
Billy Bremner
Jack Charlton
Norman Hunter
Peter Lorimer
Allan Clarke
Mick Jones
Johnny Giles
Eddie Gray

6 . ITALY'S 1982 WORLD CUP WINNERS
Zoff
Bergomi
Cabrini
Collovati
Scirea
Gentile
Oriali
Tardelli
Conti
Graziani

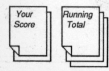

Your Score   Running Total

79 THE NAME GAME

EACH clue leads to a well-known name. Put the initials in the appropriate squares to identify a sports star: One point for each correct answer, plus a bonus of five points for completing the main name.

Average score: 4   Greavsie: 10

1	2	3	4	5	6		
7	8	9	10	11	12	13	14

9 & 5	There's a senior and a junior one of these on the Irish golfing circuit.
13 & 10	The former Arsenal manager who is Bobby Robson's right-hand man.
3 & 12	A master of the snooker table who is a former policeman.
11 & 14	This German show jumping master was faultless in the 1976 Olympics.
8 & 6	He was nicknamed 'Nasty' but was 'tasty' with a racket in his hand.
4 & 1	The Leicestershire left-hander who is always graceful at the wicket.
7 & 2	His goal for Ipswich took the biscuit in the 1978 FA Cup Final.

ANSWERS

ON A PLATE (Page 117): 1. West Ham United;   2. Gene Tunney; 3. Chester;   4. Garfield Sobers;   5. Tony Roche;   6. Ed Moses;   7. Lucius;   8. American football;   9. Nick Faldo;   10. The Oval;   11. Gary Lineker;   12. Jamaican;   13. Niki Lauda;   14. Coventry City; 15.Ivan Lendl.

Your Score   Running Total

TAKE

CARD

Take a card — any card — on each of the following 12 pages and see if you can deal yourself a winning hand. Read each of the four questions on the page and then decide which one of them you feel confident you can answer. You must be all-correct with your answer to get the points value of the card. Remember, you can score only off one card on each page.

Average score: 35
Greavsie: 47

ANSWERS

TEAM SHEET (Page 118): 1 Gordon Strachan; 2 Ferenc Puskas; 3 Emlyn Hughes; 4 Gerson; 5 David Harvey; 6 Paolo Rossi.

For 2 points:

Name the two rival captains in the World Cup Final between England and West Germany at Wembley in 1966

For 3 points:

Name three of the five boxers who challenged Rocky Marciano for the world heavyweight championship

For 4 points:

Name four of the eight golfers who have won the British Open championship more than once since the war

For 5 points:

Name five of the seven cricketers who have captained England against Australia since Ray Illingworth was skipper

ANSWERS

THE NAME GAME (Page 119): Jockey Sir GORDON RICHARDS (Christy O'Connor, Don Howe, Ray Reardon, Alvin Schockemohle, Ilie Nastase, David Gower, Roger Osborne).

For 2 points:

Name the two
National Hunt
jockeys who
rode Red Rum
to victories
in the
Grand National
at Aintree

For 3 points:

Name three
of the five
internationals
who have
won more
than 40
Rugby Union
caps with Wales

For 4 points:

Name four of
the six men
who have
managed
England's
football
team since
the war

For 5 points:

Name five of
the eight
Australians
who have won
the men's
singles title
at Wimbledon
since the war

ANSWERS

The Take A Card answers for this hand are on page 124.

For 2 points:

Name the two boxers who fought for the vacant world heavyweight title when Rocky Marciano retired in 1956

For 3 points:

Name three of the five clubs that have won the League title three or more times since the war

For 4 points:

Name four of the six British athletes who have held the world one mile record this century

For 5 points:

Name five of the ten cities that have acted as hosts to the Olympic Games since the war

ANSWERS

TAKE A CARD (Page 121): 2: Bobby Moore and Uwe Seeler; 3: Jersey Joe Walcott, Roland LaStarza, Ezzard Charles (twice); Don Cockell, Archie Moore; 4: Bobby Locke, Peter Thomson, Gary Player, Arnold Palmer, Jack Nicklaus, Lee Trevino, Tom Watson, Seve Ballesteros; 5: Mike Denness, Tony Greig, Mike Brearley, Ian Botham, Bob Willis, David Gower, Mike Gatting (John Edrich was captain for one Test).

For 2 points:

Name the two horses that were involved in the thrilling finish to the 1973 Grand National at Aintree

For 3 points:

Name three of the four clubs that have won the Scottish Premier Division since it started in 1975

For 4 points:

Name four of the seven batsmen who have scored 1,000 runs in a season on 25 or more occasions

For 5 points:

Name five of the eight non-American boxers who challenged Muhammad Ali for the world heavyweight title

ANSWERS

TAKE A CARD (Page 122): 2: Bryan Fletcher and Tommy Stack; 3: JPR Williams, Gareth Edwards, Gerald Davies, Ken Jones, Graham Price; 4: Walter Winterbottom, Alf Ramsey, Joe Mercer, Don Revie, Ron Greenwood, Bobby Robson; 5: Frank Sedgman, Lew Hoad, Ashley Cooper, Neale Fraser, Rod Laver, Roy Emerson, John Newcombe, Pat Cash.

2

For 2 points:

Name the two batsmen who between them scored 30 centuries during the summer of 1947

3

For 3 points:

Name three of the four champion show jumpers who rode these horses: Stroller, Psalm, Boomerang and Beethoven

4

For 4 points:

Name the four men who have managed West Ham in post-war football.

5

For 5 points:

Name five of the six American golfers who have won the British Open championship since 1970

Your Score

Running Total

2

For 2 points:

Name the two British sprinters who have won Olympic gold medals in the 100 metres

3

For 3 points:

Name three of the five boxers who conquered Muhammad Ali during his professional career

4

For 4 points:

Name four of the six British drivers who have won the world motor racing championship

5

For 5 points:

Name five of the nine women who have won the Wimbledon singles title more than once since the war

Your Score

Running Total

ANSWERS

TAKE A CARD (Page 124): 2: Red Rum and Crisp; 3: Rangers, Celtic, Aberdeen, Dundee United; 4: WGGrace, Frank Woolley, Colin Cowdrey, Philip Mead, Geoff Boycott, Jack Hobbs, Patsy Hendren; 5: George Chuvalo, Henry Cooper, Brian London, Karl Mildenberger, Joe Bugner, Jean-Pierre Coopman, Richard Dunn, Alfredo Evangelista.

For 2 points:

Name the two goalkeepers in the 1980 FA Cup Final between West Ham and Arsenal at Wembley

For 3 points:

Name three of the five jockeys who rode these Derby winners: Royal Palace, Blakeney, Shirley Heights, Shergar and Snow Knight

For 4 points:

Name four of the five counties that have won the County Cricket championship outright eight or more times

For 5 points:

Name five of the seven opponents Henry Cooper fought in British heavyweight title fights

For 2 points:

Name the two
athletes who
won medals
for Britain in
the 400 metres
hurdles final
at the 1968
Olympics

For 3 points:

Name three
of the four
Rugby players
who have made
12 or more
appearances
for the
British Lions

For 4 points:

Name four of
the five
clubs that
England winger
Peter Barnes
has played
for in League
matches

For 5 points:

Name five of
the eight
players who
have won
the world
snooker
championship
more than once

Your Score

Running Total

For 2 points:

Name the two
flat racing
classics
that are
staged
on the
Newmarket
course

For 3 points:

Name three
of the four
runners-up in
these football
World Cup
Finals:
1954, 1958
1962, 1970

For 4 points:

Name four of
the five
American boxers
who won Olympic
gold medals in
1976 and went
on to become
professionals

For 5 points:

Name five of
the seven
bowlers who
have taken
more than
200 Test
wickets for
England

ANSWERS

TAKE A CARD (Page 127): 2: Phil Parkes and Pat Jennings; 3: George Moore (Royal Palace), Eph Johnson (Blakeney), Greville Starkey (Shirley Heights), Walter Swinburn (Shergar), Brian Taylor (Snow Knight); 4: Yorkshire, Surrey, Notts, Middlesex, Lancashire; 5: Joe Erskine, Brian London, Dick Richardson, Johnny Prescott, Jack Bodell, Billy Walker, Joe Bugner.

For 2 points:

Name the two
darts masters
who are the
only players
to have
won the
four major
championships

For 3 points:

Name three
of the four
British-born
runners who have
set world's fastest
times for the
marathon
since the war

For 4 points:

Name four of
the five
left handed
players who
have won the
men's singles
title at Wimbledon
since the war

For 5 points:

Name five of
the six
clubs Derek
Dougan played
for during his
career in
the Football
League

Your
Score

Running
Total

ANSWERS

TAKE A CARD (Page 128): 2: David Hemery and John Sherwood; 2: Willie
John McBride, Dickie Jeeps, Mike Gibson, Graham Price; 3: Man City, West
Brom, Leeds United, Coventry City, Man United; 4: Joe Davis, Walter
Donaldson, Fred Davis, John Pulman, Ray Reardon, John Spencer, Alex
Higgins, Steve Davis.

130

For 2 points:

Name the two horses on which Lester Piggott won the Prix de l'Arc de Triomphe, winning twice on one of them

For 3 points:

Name the three British boxers who have won the world middleweight championship since the war

For 4 points:

Name four of the seven managers who have been in charge at Liverpool since the war

For 5 points:

Name five of the eight batsmen with whom Len Hutton opened for England against Australia in Test matches

ANSWERS

TAKE A CARD (Page 129): 2: 1,000 and 2,000 Guineas; 3: Hungary, Sweden, Czechoslovakia, Italy; 4. Leon Spinks, Michael Spinks, Ray Leonard, Howard Davis, Leo Randolph; 5: Ian Botham, Bob Willis, Fred Trueman, Derek Underwood, Brian Statham, Alec Bedser, John Snow.

Your Score

Running Total

For 2 points:

Name the two rival captains in the World Cup Final between West Germany and Holland in Munich in 1974

 For 3 points:

Name the three British women who have won the Wimbledon singles championship since the war

 For 4 points:

Name the four England bowlers with a surname beginning with the initial 'T' who have taken more than 75 wickets in Test cricket

 For 5 points:

Name five of the eight sprinters who have completed the double in the men's Olympic 100 and 200 metres

 Your Score

 Running Total

ANSWERS

TAKE A CARD (Page 130): 2: Eric Bristow and John Lowe; 3: Jim Peters, Basil Heatley, Derek Clayton (now an Australian), Steve Jones; 4: Jaroslav Drobny, Neale Fraser, Rod Laver, Jimmy Connors, John McEnroe; 5: Portsmouth, Blackburn Rovers, Aston Villa, Peterborough, Leicester City, Wolves.

ROUNDERS

The sports puzzle that will have you going in circles.

Each clue leads to a familiar sports word or name. The LAST letter of each word or name is the FIRST letter of the next. One point for each correct answer and a 5-point bonus if you complete the circle.
Average score: 3
Greavsie: 9

1	What a Rugby full-back must often do in defence (6).
2	Surname of the jockey who won the 1982 Derby (6).
3	You will see more than one of these at Cowes (5).
4	An international cricketer's ultimate examination (4).
5	Big Bill, who won three Wimbledon singles titles (6).
6	Fishermen and goal-hungry strikers try to fill it! (3).

ANSWERS

TAKE A CARD (Page 131): 2: Rheingold and Alleged (twice); 3: Randolph Turpin, Terry Downes, Alan Minter; 4: George Kay, Don Welsh, Phil Taylor, Bill Shankly, Bob Paisley, Joe Fagan, Kenny Dalglish; 5: Charlie Barnett (2 Tests), Bill Edrich (6), Cyril Washbrook (11), John Dewes (1), Don Kenyon (2), Reg Simpson (1), Trevor Bailey (1), Tom Graveney (1).

Your Score

Running Total

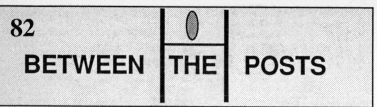

BETWEEN THE POSTS

Award yourself one point for each correct answer to the following 8 Rugby questions. Average score: 2 Greavsie: 3

1. Which All Blacks full-back beat the 1959 British Lions with six penalty goals after they had scored three tries?
a) Don Clarke; b) Bob Scott; c) George Nepia

2. Who used to play for Llanelli before switching to Rugby League and scoring 144 tries and 1,245 goals for Leeds?
a) Bev Risman; b) Lewis Jones c) David Watkins

3. With which Rugby League club did David Watkins score 200 goals and 49 tries?
a) Salford; b) Widnes; c) St Helens

4. Who was Richard Sharp's scrum-half partner when he made a stunning debut for England against Wales in 1960?
a) Nigel Starmer-Smith; b) Gus Rimmer; c) Dickie Jeeps

5. Name the Irishman who captained the triumphant British Lions in South Africa in 1974.
a) Willie-John McBride; b) Mike Gibson; c) Willie Duggan

6. Which international player scored a record five penalty goals and two conversions in the 1975 Varsity match?
a) Bob Hiller; b) Alastair Hignell; c) Chris Laidlaw

7. How many times did Gareth Edwards and Barry John play together for Wales?
a) 23; b) 33; c) 43

8. With which club side did David Duckham regularly play?
a) Harlequins; b) Coventry; c) Leicester

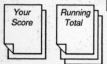
Your Score
Running Total

ANSWERS

TAKE A CARD (Page 132): 1 Franz Beckenbauer (West Germany), Johan Cruyff (Holland); 2 Angela Mortimer, Ann Jones, Virginia Wade; 3 Fred Trueman, Maurice Tate, Fred Titmus, Frank Tyson; 4 Archie Hahn, Ralph Craig; Percy Williams, Eddie Tolan, Jesse Owens, Bobby-Joe Morrow, Valeri Borzov, Carl Lewis.

83

Award yourself a point for each Test wicket-keeper that you can identify from the following clues.
Average score: 3 Greavsie 4

1. This master stumper played for Kent from 1939 until 1969. He made 219 dismissals in 91 Tests for England, and scored 2,439 Test runs including two centuries.

2. Our second wicket-keeper also played for Kent – from 1926 to 1951. He was noted as a top-flight batsman, scoring 37,248 runs during his career and averaging 40.56 in 47 Tests.

3. Once a footballer with Port Vale, this wicket-keeper held a record 1,473 catches in a 26-year career that started with Derbyshire in 1960. He played in 57 Tests and held a record 10 catches in one Test against India.

4. This Australian featured with Queensland and made 187 dismissals in 51 Tests. He held 20 catches during the memorable series against the West Indies in 1960-61.

5. A true giant of West Indian cricket, this player was more noted for his batting power than his skill behind the stumps. He averaged 56.68 runs in 44 Tests and was one of a famous trio.

6. Finally, we have an Australian who made a record 355 dismissals in 96 Tests and was an aggressive left-handed batsman for Western Australia. He will always be remembered for his partnership with Dennis Lillee.

ANSWERS

Your Score

Running Total

SPORTS NEWS EXTRA

84 HEADLINE MAKERS

Can you fill in the blanks in the following sporting headlines? Award yourself one point for each gap that you fill.
Average score: 7
Greavsie: 8

1. TYSON *OUTPOINTS BLANK TO BECOME UNDISPUTED KING*

2. WINTER RIDES BLANK TO HIS FIRST NATIONAL VICTORY

3. BLANK'S SUPER SOLO GOAL CLINCHES 1981 FA CUP FINAL WIN FOR SPURS

4. BLANK PIPS NICKLAUS BY ONE SHOT TO WIN THE 1977 BRITISH OPEN

5. BLANK WINS 1980 OLYMPIC 100 METRES SPRINT BY JUST INCHES

6. BLANK COMPLETES FIRST FA CUP FINAL HAT-TRICK AS BLACKPOOL BEAT BOLTON AT WEMBLEY

7. BLANK'S UNBEATEN 149 LIFTS ENGLAND TO HEADINGLEY WIN

8. IRISHMAN BLANK SCORES RECORD 38 TRIES FOR BRITISH LIONS

9. *MARTINA CONQUERS BLANK TO WIN HER EIGHTH WIMBLEDON TITLE*

10. 'I KNEW I HAD IT WON WHEN WE CAME OFF THE MOUNTAINS' SAYS 1987 TOUR WINNER BLANK

11. BLANK SCORES 18 IN THE FINAL OVER FOR A ONE-DAY WIN OVER THE AUSSIES

12. BLANK FIRST TO BEAT FRAZIER

13. BLANK WINS 800 METRES FOR BRITAIN IN TOKYO

14. ENGLAND BEAT BLANK 9-3 AT WEMBLEY

ANSWERS

Your Score
Running Total

BETWEEN THE POSTS (Page 134): 1 Don Clarke; 2 Lewis Jones; 3 Salford; 4 Dickie Jeeps; 5 Willie-John McBride; 6 Alastair Hignell; 7 23 times; 8 Coventry.

85

SECONDS OUT!

You have got to go 10 rounds with 10 different world boxing champions from the past. Award yourself one point each time you can identify your opponent. Give yourself a five point knockout bonus if you can name 7 or more.
Average score: 5 Greavsie: 6

Round 1: This Irishman was world flyweight champion in the 1940s and used to sing 'When Irish Eyes Are Smiling' in the ring.

Round 2: A deaf mute, this Italian took the world bantamweight title from Robert Cohen in 1956. They used to flash lights to signal the bell had gone.

Round 3: Your featherweight opponent is a Panamanian who lost his championship to Barry McGuigan at Shepherds Bush in 1985.

Round 4: Now you're in against a lightweight champion who took the title from Scottish idol Jim Watt.

Round 5: Coming out from the light-welterweight corner is the hero of the New York Latin Quarter who knocked out Maurice Hope in 1981.

Round 6: This fighter ended John Stracey's reign as welterweight champion and knocked out Dave 'Boy' Green.

Round 7: Your light-middleweight opponent is the 1976 Olympic champion who ended the title reign at 11st 6lbs of Marvin Hagler.

Round 8: The Argentinian who was world champion for seven years in the 1970s comes out fighting for the middleweights.

Round 9: This light-heavyweight champion worked as a sheriff in Albuquerque and included Chris Finnegan among his victims.

Round 10: Finally, you are matched against the former world heavyweight champion who was born in Brandenburg.

ANSWERS

HOWZAT (Page 135): 1 Godfrey Evans; 2 Les Ames; 3 Bob Taylor; 4 Wally Grout; 5 Clyde Walcott; 6 Rodney Marsh.

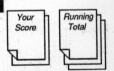

Your Score

Running Total

86 GUESS THE GUEST

See how quickly you can identify
a star sportsman from the clues.
Average score: 6   Greavsie: 10

For 12 points: Our mystery guest was born in Heswall, Cheshire, on November 24, 1955. His father was serving with the Fleet Air Arm and he moved to Northern Ireland at the age of two.

For 10 points: Following his father's retirement from the Royal Navy, the family moved to Yeovil which was where he started his sporting career.

For 8 points: He was offered a career in football by Crystal Palace manager Bert Head, but he decided to follow a different sporting path.

For 6 points: On leaving school, he was taken on the Lord's ground staff and was registered to play County cricket for Somerset.

For 4 points: An all-rounder, he won a place in the Somerset side in 1974 and came under the influence of skipper Brian Close.

For 2 points: He has since become the world's leading Test wicket-taker and has thrilled cricket spectators around the world with his hurricane hitting in more than 90 Test matches for England. Now plays for Worcestershire.

Your Score

Running Total

ROUNDERS

The sports puzzle that will have you going in circles.

Each clue leads to a familiar sports word or name. The LAST letter of each word or name is the FIRST letter of the next. One point for each correct answer and a 5-point bonus if you complete the circle.
Average score: 4
Greavsie: 8

1	Boxers do this in the gym when training for a fight (4).
2	The sport at which Prince Obolensky shone (5).
3	Terry, who skippered Wales and Coventry City (6).
4	They have never been a barrier to Ed Moses! (7).
5	Colin Cowdrey held many catches in this position (4).
6	Gareth Edwards and Johnny Haynes made it best (4).

ANSWERS

SECONDS OUT (Page 137): 1 Rinty Monoghan; 2 Mario D'Agata; 3 Eusebio Pedroza; 4 Alexis Arguello; 5 Wilfred Benitez; 6 Carlos Palomino; 7 Sugar Ray Leonard; 8 Carlos Monzon; 9 Bob Foster; 10 Max Schmeling.

Your Score | Running Total

THE COMPUTER RATINGS GAME

On the following 11 pages you can match your sports knowledge and opinions against a computer. We have fed into a computer facts and figures (and added personal feelings) on the 12 top champions in several sports. We have listed them in alphabetical order. All you have to do is number the champions in the order that you rate them, taking skill, achievement, experience and physical attributes into account. For instance, in the boxing if you consider Muhammad Ali to have been No.1 put a figure '1' in the box alongside his name, then a '2' alongside your second-rated boxer and rate them all from 1-12. Then compare your list with the computer rating answers and award yourself one point each time your rating matches that of the computer.

COMPUTER RATINGS BOXING

There are 12 old-time world heavyweight champions listed below in alphabetical order. See if your ratings of them match the computer. Award yourself one point each time your rating is the same.
Average score: 4 Greavsie: 5

1 Max Baer

2 Tommy Burns

3 Primo Carnera

4 James J.Corbett

5 Jack Dempsey

6 James J. Jeffries

7 Jack Johnson

8 Max Schmeling

9 Jack Sharkey

10 John L. Sullivan

11 Gene Tunney

12 Jess Willard

ANSWERS

ROUNDERS (Page 139): 1. Spar; 2. Rugby; 3. Yorath; 4. Hurdles; 5. slip; 6. Pass — SpaRugbYoratHurdleSliPasS.

Your Score

Running Total

COMPUTER RATINGS BOXING

There are 12 modern world heavyweight champions listed below in alphabetical order. See if your ratings of them match the computer. Award yourself one point each time your rating is the same.
Average score: 5   Greavsie: 6

1 Ezzard Charles

2 George Foreman

3 Joe Frazier

4 Larry Holmes

5 Ingemar Johansson

6 Sonny Liston

7 Joe Louis

8 Rocky Marciano

9 Muhammad Ali

10 Floyd Patterson

11 Mike Tyson

12 Joe Walcott

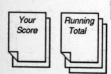

Your Score

Running Total

ANSWERS

The answers for the heavyweight computer ratings are on page 144

142

There are 12 top Test batsman of last 30 years listed below in alphabetical order. See if your ratings of them match the computer. Award yourself one point each time your rating is the same.

Average score: 4 Greavsie: 6

1 Allan Border

2 Geoff Boycott

3 Greg Chappell

4 Sunil Gavaskar

5 David Gower

6 Gordon Greenidge

7 Clive Lloyd

8 Javed Miandad

9 Graeme Pollock

10 Barry Richards

11 Viv Richards

12 Gary Sobers

ANSWERS

COMPUTER RATINGS, BOXING (Page 141): 1. Jack Johnson; 2. GeneTunney; 3. Jack Dempsey; 4. James J. Jeffries; 5. James J. Corbett; 6. John L. Sullivan; 7. Tommy Burns; 8. Jess Willard; 9. Max Schmeling; 10. Max Baer; 11. Primo Carnera; 12. Jack Sharkey.

Your Score

Running Total

COMPUTER RATINGS CRICKET

There are 12 top fast bowlers of the last 30 years listed below in alphabetical order. See if your ratings of them match the computer. Award yourself one point each time your rating is the same.
Average score: 5   Greavsie: 6

1 Richard Hadlee
2 Wes Hall
3 Michael Holding
4 Imran Khan
5 Dennis Lillee
6 Malcolm Marshall
7 Graham McKenzie
8 Mike Procter
9 John Snow
10 Jeff Thomson
11 Fred Trueman
12 Bob Willis

ANSWERS

Your Score   Running Total

COMPUTER RATINGS, BOXING (Page 142): 1. Joe Louis; 2. Muhammad Ali; 3. Rocky Marciano; 4. Larry Holmes; 5. Mike Tyson; 6. George Foreman; 7. Sonny Liston; 8. Joe Frazier; 9. Jersey Joe Walcott; 10. Ezzard Charles; 11. Floyd Patterson; 12. Ingemar Johansson.

COMPUTER RATINGS CRICKET

There are 12 top all-rounders of the last 20 years listed below in alphabetical order. See if your ratings of them match the computer. Award yourself one point each time your rating is the same.

Average score: 4 Greavsie: 7

1 Asif Iqbal

2 Eddie Barlow

3 Ian Botham

4 Keith Boyce

5 Tony Greig

6 Richard Hadlee

7 Imran Khan

8 Kapil Dev

9 Mustaq Mohammad

10 Mike Procter

11 Ravi Shastri

12 Gary Sobers

ANSWERS

COMPUTER RATINGS, CRICKET (Page 143): 1. Gary Sobers; 2. Viv Richards; 3. Barry Richards; 4. Greg Chappell; 5. Graeme Pollock; 6. Sunil Gavaskar; 7. Geoff Boycott; 8. Allan Border; 9. Clive Lloyd; 10. Gordon Greenidge; 11. Javed Miandad; 12. David Gower.

Your Score

Running Total

COMPUTER RATINGS GOLF

There are 12 modern golfers listed below in alphabetical order. See if your ratings of them match the computer. Award yourself one point each time your rating is the same.
Average score: 4 Greavsie: 5

1 Seve Ballesteros
2 Ben Hogan
3 Bobby Locke
4 Johnny Miller
5 Jack Nicklaus
6 Greg Norman
7 Arnold Palmer
8 Gary Player
9 Sam Snead
10 Peter Thomson
11 Lee Trevino
12 Tom Watson

ANSWERS

Your Score

Running Total

COMPUTER RATINGS, CRICKET (Page 144): 1. Dennis Lillee; 2. Malcolm Marshall; 3. Fred Trueman; 4. Michael Holding; 5. Wes Hall; 6. Richard Hadlee; 7. Imran Khan; 8. Jeff Thomson; 9. Bob Willis; 10. Mike Procter; 11. Graham McKenzie; 12. John Snow.

COMPUTER RATINGS TENNIS

There are 12 top post-war men's tennis players listed below in alphabetical order. See if your ratings of them match the computer. Award yourself one point each time your rating is the same.
Average score: 3   Greavsie: 5

1	Boris Becker	
2	Bjorn Borg	
3	Jimmy Connors	
4	Pancho Gonzales	
5	Lew Hoad	
6	Jack Kramer	
7	Rod Laver	
8	Ivan Lendl	
9	John McEnroe	
10	John Newcombe	
11	Ken Rosewall	
12	Frank Sedgman	

ANSWERS

COMPUTER RATINGS, CRICKET (Page 145): 1.Gary Sobers; 2. Ian Botham; 3. Imran Khan; 4. Richard Hadlee; 5. Mike Procter; 6. Kapil Dev; 7. Tony Greig; 8. Eddie Barlow; 9. Mustaq Mohammad; 10. Asif Iqbal; 11. Keith Boyce; 12. Ravi Shastri.

Your Score

Running Total

COMPUTER RATINGS TENNIS

There are 12 top post-war women's tennis players listed below in alphabetical order. See if your ratings of them match the computer. Award yourself one point each time your rating is the same.

Average score: 4 Greavsie: 5

1 Pauline Betz
2 Louise Brough
3 Maria Bueno
4 Evonne Cawley
5 Mo Connolly
6 Margaret Court
7 Margaret Du Pont
8 Chris Evert
9 Althea Gibson
10 Doris Hart
11 Billie-Jean King
12 Martina Navratilova

ANSWERS

COMPUTER RATINGS, GOLF (Page 146): 1. Jack Nicklaus; 2. Ben Hogan; 3. Tom Watson; 4. Arnold Palmer; 5. Gary Player; 6. Sam Snead; 7. Seve Ballesteros; 8. Lee Trevino; 9. Greg Norman; 10. Johnny Miller; 11. Peter Thomson; 12. Bobby Locke.

COMPUTER RATINGS FOOTBALL

There are the 12 most successful post-war football clubs listed below in alphabetical order. See if your ratings of them match the computer. Award yourself one point each time your rating is the same.

Average score: 6 Greavsie: 8

1 Arsenal	
2 Aston Villa	
3 Derby County	
4 Everton	
5 Ipswich Town	
6 Leeds United	
7 Liverpool	
8 Manchester City	
9 Manchester United	
10 Nottingham Forest	
11 Tottenham Hotspur	
12 Wolves	

ANSWERS

COMPUTER RATINGS, TENNIS (Page 147): 1. Rod Laver; 2. Bjom Borg; 3. John McEnroe; 4. Jack Kramer; 5. Pancho Gonzales; 6. Lew Hoad; 7. Ivan Lendl; 8. Ken Rosewall; 9. Frank Sedgman; 10. Boris Becker; 11. John Newcombe 12. Jimmy Connors.

Your Score

Running Total

COMPUTER RATINGS MILERS

There are 12 mile and metric mile runners who have held the world record in the last 30 years listed below in alphabetical order. See if your ratings of them match the computer. Award yourself one point each time your rating is the same.

Average score: 4 Greavsie: 6

1 Said Aouita	
2 Filbert Bayi	
3 Seb Coe	
4 Steve Cram	
5 Herb Elliott	
6 Derek Ibbotson	
7 Michel Jazy	
8 Sidney Maree	
9 Steve Ovett	
10 Jim Ryun	
11 Peter Snell	
12 John Walker	

Your Score   Running Total

ANSWERS

COMPUTER RATINGS, TENNIS (Page 148): 1.Martina Navratilova; 2.Mo Connolly; 3.Margaret Court; 4. Billie-Jean King; 5. Chris Evert; 6. Maria Bueno; 7. Louise Brough; 8. Evonne Cawley; 9. Margaret Du Pont; 10. Althea Gibson; 11 Pauline Betz; 12. Doris Hart.

COMPUTER RATINGS SNOOKER

There are 12 top snooker players listed below in alphabetical order. See if your ratings of them match the computer. Award yourself one point each time your rating is the same.

Average score: 3 Greavsie: 4

1 Fred Davis

2 Joe Davis

3 Steve Davis

4 Terry Griffiths

5 Alex Higgins

6 Joe Johnson

7 John Pulman

8 Ray Reardon

9 John Spencer

10 Dennis Taylor

11 Cliff Thorburn

12 Jimmy White

ANSWERS

COMPUTER RATINGS, FOOTBALL (Page 149); 1. Liverpool; 2. Manchester United; 3. Everton; 4. Tottenham Hotspur; 5. Arsenal; 6. Leeds United; 7. Wolves; 8. Nottingham Forest; 9. Aston Villa; 10. Manchester City; 11. Derby County; 12. Ipswich Town.

Your Score

Running Total

HOW WELL D'YOU KNOW...?
PETER SHILTON

*Award yourself one point for each question
you can answer about Peter Shilton.*
Average score: 6   Greavsie: 7

1. With which club did he start his Football League career?

2. Who was the goalkeeper he succeeded when he first came into the League team?

3. Against which club did he appear in the 1969 FA Cup Final at Wembley?

4. In which year was he transferred for the first time?

5. Which manager signed him for his second club?

6. Who was his manager when he moved to his third club?

7. How old was he when he made his international debut?

8. Which England manager selected him for his first match?

9. Name the home ground of his fourth League club.

10. Which manager signed him for Derby County?

ANSWERS

Your
Score

Running
Total

COMPUTER RATINGS, MILERS (Page 150): 1 Herb Elliott; 2
Sebastian Coe; 3 Steve Cram; 4 Said Aouita; 5 John Walker; 6 Peter
Snell; 7 Steve Ovett; 8 Jim Ryun; 9 Filbert Bayi; 10 Michel Jazy; 11
Sydney Maree; 12 Derek Ibbotson.

HOW WELL D'YOU KNOW...?
MUHAMMAD ALI

Award yourself one point for each question you can answer about Muhammad Ali
Average score: 5 Greavsie: 7

1. Where was he born?

2. What was his full name at birth?

3. At which Olympics did he win a gold medal as a light-heavyweight?

4. In which year and at which venue was he knocked down by Henry Cooper in a non-title fight?

5. From whom did he first take the world heavyweight title?

6. Who did he beat in the 'Thriller in Manila'?

7. In which country did he knock out George Foreman?

8. How many professional fights did he have?

9. At the end of which round did he retire against Larry Holmes?

10. Who was his opponent in his last fight?

ANSWERS

COMPUTER RATINGS, SNOOKER (Page 151): 1 Joe Davis; 2 Steve Davis; 3 Ray Reardon; 4 Alex Higgins; 5 Cliff Thorburn; 6 John Pullman; 7 John Spencer; 8 Terry Griffiths; 9 Dennis Taylor; 10 Jimmy White; 11 Fred Davis; 12 Joe Johnson.

Your Score

Running Total

HOW WELL D'YOU KNOW...?
ARNOLD PALMER

Award yourself one point for each question you can answer about Arnold Palmer
Average score: 4 Greavsie: 6

1. In which State was he born?

2. Which was his first triumph in a major tournament?

3. How many times did he win the British Open?

4. On which course did he win his first British Open?

5. Who beat him in a play-off for the US Open in 1962?

6. What name is given to the fans who follow him around the world's fairways?

7. In which year did he score his last victory in a major tournament?

8. How many times did he win the US Masters title?

9. Which is the one major title that has always eluded him?

10. Who beat him by one shot in the 1960 British Open?

Your
Score

Running
Total

ANSWERS

HOW WELL D'YOU KNOW PETER SHILTON (Page 152): 1 Leicetser City; 2 Gordon Banks; 3 Manchester City; 4 1974; 5 Tony Waddington (Stoke City); 6 Brian Clough (Nottingham Forest); 7 21; 8 Alf Ramsey; 9 The Dell (Southampton); 10 Arthur Cox.

Award yourself one point for each question you can answer about George Best
Average score: 6 Greavsie: 8

1. In which year was he born?

2. Who was the first manager to select him for a League match?

3. Against which club did he score six FA Cup tie goals in his comeback match after a suspension?

4. In which year was he voted Europe's Player of the Year?

5. Against which club did he play in a European Cup Final?

6. For which club did he play in Los Angeles?

7. Who was club captain when he played for Fulham?

8. How many Northern Ireland caps did he win?

9. With which Fourth Division club did he play in 1975?

10. How many League championship medals did he win?

ANSWERS

HOW WELL D'YOU KNOW MUHAMMAD ALI (apge 153): 1 Louisville, Kentucky; 2 Cassius Marcellus Clay; 3 Rome, 1960; 4 1963, Wembley Stadium; 5 Sonny Liston; 6 Joe Frazier; 7 Zaire; 8 61 fights; 9 10th round; 10 Trevor Berbick (lost points 10 rounds, 1981.

Your Score

Running Total

HOW WELL D'YOU KNOW...?
LESTER PIGGOTT

*Award yourself one point
for each question that you
can answer about
Lester Piggott.*
Average score: 5
Greavsie: 7

1. In which year was he born?

2. At which age did he ride his first winner?

3. On which horse did he win his first 2,000 Guineas race?

4. How many classic winners did he ride during his career?

5. Who owned his 1957 Oaks winner Carrozza?

6. How many times was he champion jockey?

7. On which horse did he first win the St Leger?

8. With which trainer was he most closely associated until becoming a freelance rider?

9. Name his third Washington International winner.

10. Whose all-time classics record did he overtake in 1984?

Your Score

Running Total

ANSWERS

HOW WELL D'YOU KNOW ARNOLD PALMER (Page 154): 1 Pennsylvania; 2 US Masters, 1958; 3 Twice (1961, 1962); 4 Royal Birkdale; 5 Jack Nicklaus; 6 Arnie's Army; 7 1964, US Masters; 8 Four times; 9 USPGA; 10 Kel Nagle.

HOW WELL D'YOU KNOW...?
PELE

Award yourself one point for each question you can answer about Pele.
Average score: 5
Greavsie: 7

1. With which Brazilian club did he play for 19 years?

2. In which year did he first play in the World Cup finals?

3. How old was he at the time of his World Cup debut?

4. Against which side did he play his first World Cup Final?

5. Against which side did he play his last World Cup Final?

6. In how many World Cup final tournaments did he play?

7. With which club did he become an idol in the North American Soccer League?

8. Which number shirt did he always wear?

9. How many full internationals caps did he win?

10. Against which country was he carried off injured during the 1966 World Cup finals in England?

ANSWERS

HOW WELL D'YOU KNOW GEORGE BEST (Page 155): 1 1946; 2 Matt Busby; 3 Northampton Town; 4 1968; 5 Benfica; 6 The Aztecs; 7 Alan Mullery; 8 37 caps; 9 Stockport County; 10 Two League Championship medals.

Your Score

Running Total

HOW WELL D'YOU KNOW...?
TORVILL & DEAN

Award yourself one point for each question you can answer about ice skaters Jayne Torvill and Christopher Dean.
Average score: 4 Greavsie: 5

1. In which English city did they first start their partnership?

2. What did Christopher do for a living before turning full time to ice skating?

3. Is Christopher or Jayne the eldest of the partners?

4. How many British ice dance titles did they win?

5. In which year did they complete the 'Grand Slam' of World, Olympic and European championships?

6. From which show did they take their popular routine featuring a circus theme?

7. Which entertainer helped them with the routine?

8. In which championship staged in Ottawa did they set a record of 29 perfect six marks?

9. What was their famous ice dance to a Ravel tune?

10. Name the award-winning show they made for ITV.

Your Score

Running Total

HOW WELL D'YOU KNOW...?
ROGER BANNISTER

Award yourself one point for each question you can answer about Roger Bannister
Average score: 5 Greavsie: 6

1. Whose world record did he break when he first ran a sub-four minute mile?

2. What was his exact time?

3. On which track did he make his historic run?

4. Who were his two principal pacemakers in the race?

5. Which title did he win in his next major race?

6. Name his arch rival from Australia who he beat in the championship race.

7. In which position did he finish in the 1,500 metres final in the 1952 Olympics?

8. How many sub-four minute miles did he run?

9. Which title did he win in his final race?

10. What is his profession?

ANSWERS

HOW WELL D'YOU KNOW PELE: 1 Santos; 2 1958; 3 17; 4 Sweden; 5 Italy; 6 Four; 7 New York Cosmos; 8 Number 10; 9 111; 10 Portugal.

Your Score

Running Total

HOW WELL D'YOU KNOW...?
JACK NICKLAUS

Award yourself one point for each question you can answer about Jack Nicklaus
Average score: 5
Greavsie: 6

1. Where was he born?

2. When did he win his first British Open?

3. Which was his first major championship victory?

4. Which title did he win in 1965 by nine strokes from joint runners-up Arnold Palmer and Gary Player?

5. On which course has he won two British Opens?

6. Who did he beat by one shot for the 1963 US Masters?

7. How many times has he won the British Open?

8. From whom did he take over as winner of most major championships in 1975?

9. How old was he when he turned professional?

10. Which record did he equal during the 1980 US Open?

Your Score

Running Total

ANSWERS

HOW WELL D'YOU KNOW TORVILL & DEAN: 1 Nottingham; 1 He was a policeman; 3 Jayne (by 9 months); 4 Six; 5 1984; 6 Barnum; 7 Michael Crawford; 8 1984 World championships; 9 The Bolero; 10 Fire and Ice.

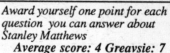

HOW WELL D'YOU KNOW...?

STANLEY MATTHEWS

Award yourself one point for each question you can answer about Stanley Matthews
Average score: 4 Greavsie: 7

1. Where was he born?

2. In which sport was his father a noted professional?

3. Which number shirt did he always wear?

4. With which club did he win his only FA Cup winners' medal at Wembley?

5. In which year did he win his medal?

6. Which team provided the opposition in the match that became known as 'the Matthews Final'?

7. How many full international caps did he win?

8. Against which country did he score his only hat-trick?

9. In which year was he voted the first ever European Footballer of the Year?

10. With which League club was he general manager following his retirement in 1965?

ANSWERS

HOW WELL D'YOU KNOW ROGER BANNISTER: 1 Gundar Haegg; 2. 3 minutes 59.4 seconds; 3 Iffley Road, Oxford; 4 Chris Brasher and Chris Chataway; 5 Empire (Commonwealth) Games mile title; 6 John Landy; 7 Fourth; 8 Two; 9 1954 European 1500 metres title; 10 Doctor (he is a leading neurologist).

Your Score

Running Total

90 WHO DID WHAT?

There are 10 points at stake in this Who's Who test, one point for each correct answer. Each answer is a surname that starts with the same initial.
Average score: 6   Greavsie: 7

1. WHO was the spin bowler who took 8 wickets for 2 runs for England against The Rest in 1950?

2. WHO won the world professional darts championship in 1979 and 1987?

3. WHO was Wimbledon men's singles champion four times in the 1960s?

4. WHO was the Austrian who won the world motor racing championship in 1975, 1977 and 1984?

5. WHO won the 1985 US Masters golf championship?

6. WHO is the highest Australian Test wicket taker?

7. WHO rode Mysterious to victory in the 1973 Oaks?

8. WHO has produced the best long jump at sea-level — but still short of Bob Beamon's 1968 leap at altitude?

9. WHO was the Scottish international who was voted European Footballer Of The Year in 1964?

10. WHO was the former world heavyweight champion stopped in eight rounds by Rocky Marciano in 1951?

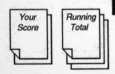

Your Score

Running Total

ANSWERS

HOW WELL D'YOU KNOW JACK NICKLAUS Page 160): 1 Columbus, Ohio; 2 1966; 3. US Open, 1962; 4 US Masters; 5 St Andrews; 6 Tony Lema; 7 Three times; 8 Bobby Jones; 9 19; 10 Lowest round of 63.

91
ODD MAN OUT

Who is the odd man out in each of the following six lists? We give you a little 'think hint' to help. Award yourself one point for each correct answer.
Average score: 3 Greavsie: 5

1. England cricketers Len Hutton, Cyril Washbrook, Brian Statham, Geoff Boycott, John Edrich, Chris Broad, Graham Gooch. *Think openers.*

2. British boxers Randolph Turpin, Terry Downes, Alan Minter, Kevin Finnegan, Peter Keenan, Tony Sibson, Mark Kaylor. *Think middles.*

3. Football managers Cliff Britton, John Carey, Harry Catterick, Jimmy Melia, Billy Bingham, Howard Kendall, Colin Harvey. *Think Goodison.*

4. Track athletes Jesse Owens, Carl Lewis, Valeri Borzov, Rod Dixon, Haseley Crawford, Don Quarrie, Allan Wells. *Think sprinters.*

5. Jockeys Bill Williamson, Tim Norman, Fred Winter, Pat Taffe, Johnny Francome, Bryan Fletcher, Tommy Stack. *Think jumpers!*

6. Golfers Seve Ballesteros, Tom Watson, Jack Nicklaus, Tony Jacklin, Arnold Palmer, Gary Player, Ben Crenshaw. *Think US Masters.*

ANSWERS

HOW WELL D'YOU KNOW STANLEY MATTHEWS (Page 161): 1 Hanley, Staffs.; 2 Boxing; 3 Seven; 4 Blackpool; 5 1953; 6 Bolton Wanderers; 7 54; 8 Czechoslovakia; 9 1956; 10 Port Vale.

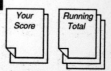

Your Score

Running Total

92 THE NAME GAME

EACH clue leads to a well-known name. Put the initials in the appropriate squares to identify a sports star: One point for each correct answer, plus a bonus of five points for completing the main name.

Average score: 6   Greavsie: 8

1	2	3	4	5				

6	7	8	9	10	11	12	13	14

9 & 7	He won the men's singles title at Wimbledon in 1964 and 1965.
4 & 8	The American sprinter who won the women's 100 metres in the LA Games.
12 & 14	He was the famous man in black in the Russian goal during the 1950s.
3 & 10	The Italian-born England all-rounder who captained England in 30 Tests.
11 & 5	This Irishman cycled to victory in the 1987 Tour de France.
1 & 13	He piloted Scintillate to victory in the 1979 Oaks.
2 & 6	The bespectacled South African who batted and bowled for Derbyshire.

Your Score

Running Total

ANSWERS

WHO DID WHAT (Page 162): 1 Jim Laker; 2 John Lowe; 3 Rod Laver; 4 Niki Lauda; 5 Bernhard Langer; 6 Dennis Lillee; 7 Geoff Lewis; 8 Carl Lewis; 9 Denis Law; 10 Joe Louis.

93

ON A PLATE

Here are 15 easy questions to help you boost your score. Award yourself a point for each correct answer, plus a one point bonus every time you get three successive questions right.
Average score: 12 Greavsie: 15

1. Which team is at home at Loftus Road?

2. Who took the world middleweight title from Terry Downes ?

3. With which club did Charlie Nicholas start his career?

4. Which horse won the Epsom Derby in 1981?

5. How many times has Tom Watson won the British Open?

6. Who won the world snooker championship in 1980?

7. Which darts player is nicknamed the 'Limestone Cowboy?'

8. Which Irishman fought Jim Watt for the world title?

9. With which sport do you associate the name David Bryant?

10. On which ground do Scotland play home football matches?

11. Who succeeded Clive Lloyd as captain of the West Indies?

12. Who was England's goalkeeper in the 1962 World Cup?

13. At which sport was Peter Collins a world champion?

14. Who took the world 9-stone title from Barry McGuigan?

15. What nationality is cricketer Kapil Dev?

ANSWERS

ODD MAN OUT (Page 163): 1 Brian Statham (was not an opening batsman); 2 Peter Keenan (was a bantamweight, not a middleweight); 3 Jimmy Melia (did not manage Everton); 4 Rod Dixon (was not a sprinter); 5 Bill Williamson (was not a jump jockey); 6 Tony Jacklin (did not win the US Masters title).

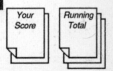

Your Score | Running Total

£££

94 THE TRANSFER TRAIL

£££

How closely do you follow the football transfer market? Here are 50 of the major deals since the first £1,000 deal in 1905 had critics muttering that the game had gone mad. In each deal we have missed out either the selling or buying club. Award yourself one point for each blank that you can fill. Average score: 24. Greavsie: 33

FEE	PLAYER	FROM	TO	YEAR
£1,000	**Alf Common**		Middlesbro'	1905
£10,890	**David Jack**	Bolton		1928
£20,000	**Tommy Lawton**		Notts Co.	1947
£30,000	**Trevor Ford**	Aston Villa		1950
£35,000	**Cliff Jones**		Tottenham	1958
£45,000	**Albert Quixall**		Man. Utd.	1958
£55,000	**Denis Law**		Man. City	1960
£100,000	**Denis Law**	Man. City to		1961
£150,000	**Allan Clarke**		Leics. City	1968
£200,000	**Martin Peters**	West Ham		1970
£220,000	**Alan Ball**		Arsenal	1971
£250,000	**David Nish**	Leicester City		1972
£300,000	**Graeme Souness**		Rangers	1986
£300,000	**Cyrille Regis**		Coventry	1984
£325,000	**Allan Simonsen**	Barcelona		1982

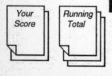

Your Score | Running Total

ANSWERS

NAME GAME (Page 164): Footballer PETER BEARDSLEY (Roy Emerson, Evelyn Ashford, Lev Yashin, Ted Dexter, Stephen Roche, Pat Eddery, Eddie Barlow).

FEE	PLAYER	FROM	TO	YEAR
£325,000	**John Gidman** Everton			1981
£330,000	**Colin Todd** Derby County			1978
£350,000	**Sammy McIlroy**		Stoke City	1982
£350,000	**Asa Hartford** Everton			1981
£350,000	**Bob Latchford**		Everton	1974
£400,000	**Paul Allen**		Tottenham	1985
£400,000	**Mickey Thomas** Everton			1981
£400,000	**Kenny Burns** Nottm Forest			1981
£400,000	**Kevin Keegan**		Southampton	1980
£400,000	**Tony Currie** Leeds United			1979
£440,000	**Kenny Dalglish**		Liverpool	1977
£450,000	**John Wark**		Liverpool	1984
£450,000	**Peter Ward** Brighton			1980
£450,000	**Brian Talbot** Ipswich Town			1979
£450,000	**Gordon McQueen**		Man.Utd	1978
£475,000	**Clive Allen**		QPR	1981
£500,000	**Tommy Caton**		Arsenal	1983
£500,000	**Tony Woodcock**		Arsenal	1982

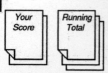

FEE	PLAYER	FROM	TO	YEAR
£500,000	**Andy Ritchie**	Man United		1980
£550,000	**Luther Blissett**		Watford	1984
£565,000	**Phil Parkes**		West Ham	1979
£600,000	**Liam Brady**	Arsenal		1980
£600,000	**Garth Crooks**		Tottenham	1980
£700,000	**Adrian Heath**		Everton	1982
£800,000	**Gary Lineker**		Everton	1985
£830,000	**Steve Archibald**		Spurs	1980
£950,000	**Laurie Cunningham**	WBA		1979
£1,000,000	**Justin Fashanu**	Norwich		1981
£1,180,000	**Trevor Francis**		Nottm.F.	1979
£1,250,000	**Garry Birtles**	Nottm For.		1980
£1,250,000	**Kevin Reeves**		Man. City	1980
£1,350,000	**Kenny Sansom**		Arsenal	1980
£1,500,000	**Ray Wilkins**	Man.United		1984
£1,500,000	**Bryan Robson**		Man. Utd	1981
£3,200,000	**Ian Rush**	Liverpool		1987

ANSWERS

THE TRANSFER TRAIL (Page 166): Common (Sunderland); Jack (Arsenal); Lawton (Chelsea); Ford (Sunderland); Jones (Swansea); Quixall (Sheff. W); Law (Huddersfield); Law (Torino); Clarke (Fulham); Peters (Spurs); Ball (Everton); Nish (Derby); Souness (Sampdoria); Regis (WBA); Simonsen (Charlton).

95

ROUNDERS

The sports puzzle that will have you going in circles.

Each clue leads to a familiar sports word or name. The LAST letter of each word or name is the FIRST letter of the next. One point for each correct answer and a 5-point bonus if you complete the circle.
Average score: 4
Greavsie: 10

1	Surname of England's youngest 1966 hero (4).
2	Middlesex are at home at this ground (5).
3	Sam, the first golfer to break 60 in a major event (5).
4	There are at least 180 reasons for knowing this game (5)
5	Sandy, who had five famous fights with Willie Pep (7).
6	George, a teacher who played for Spurs and England(4).

ANSWERS

TRANSFER TRAIL (Page 167): Gidman (Man United); Todd (Everton); McIlroy (Man U); Hartford (Man City); Latchford (Birmingham); Allen (West Ham); Thomas (Brighton); Burns (Leeds); Keegan (Hamburg); Currie (QPR); Dalglish (Celtic); Wark (Ipswich); Ward (Nottm For.); Talbot (Arsenal); McQueen (Leeds); Allen (Palace); Caton (Man City); Woodcock (Cologne).

Your Score

Running Total

*See how quickly you can identify
a star sportsman from the clues.*
Average score: 6   Greavsie: 10

For 12 points: Our mystery guest was born in London on September 29, 1956, and moved to Yorkshire as a youngster. He started his sports career in Sheffield.

For 10 points: At 14, he won the Yorkshire schools cross-country championship and two years later the English schools 3,000 metres title.

For 8 points: Coached by his father, his first major victory was in the 1977 European indoor 800 metres final.

For 6 points: On leaving school, he studied at Loughborough College where he developed into one of the world's greatest middle-distance runners.

For 4 points: He set the first of a succession of world records in Oslo in 1980 when winning the 800 metres in 1 minute 42.4 seconds.

For 2 points: Beaten by arch rival Steve Ovett in the 1980 Olympic 800 metres final, he quickly gained revenge by winning the 1,500 metres gold medal. Four years later in Los Angeles he became the first athlete to retain the 1,500 metres championship.

Your Score

Running Total

ANSWERS

TRANSFER TRAIL (Page 168): Ritchie (Brighton); Blissett (AC Mllan); Parkes (QPR); Brady (Juventus); Crooks (Stoke City); Heath (Stoke City); Lineker (Leicester); Archibald (Aberdeen); Cunningham (Real Madrid); Fashanu (Nottm For.); Francis (Birmingham); Birtles (Man U.); Reeves (Norwich); Sansom (Palace); Wilkins (AC Milan) Robson (WBA), Rush (Juventus).

Untangle the letters in each of the sections to identify famous sports personalities. Award yourself two points for each correct identification.

Average score: 4 Greavsie: 6

1. Clue: He knows how to be mean!

2. Clue: Try this cricketer for openers.

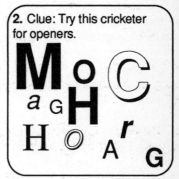

3. Clue: She is courting a lot of publicity.

4. Clue: He was a big smoker when in action.

ROUNDERS (Page 169): 1 (Alan) Ball; 2 Lord's; 3 (Sam) Snead; 4 Darts; 5 (Sandy) Saddler; 6 (George) Robb — BalLordSneaDartSaddleRobb

Your Score

Running Total

98

CLUB CALL

How well d'you know
the League champions?

Fifteen clubs have won the Football League Championship during the post-war years. How well d'you know them? There are 10 questions on each of the clubs on the following pages. Award yourself one point for each question that you get right.

Average score: 76 Greavsie: 87

First of all, for starters: How many of the 15 championship-winning clubs can you name? One point for each correct answer. Average score: 10. Greavsie: 14

(These points are in addition to the Club Call score)

Your Score

Running Total

ANSWERS

GUESS THE GUEST (Page 170): Our mystery personality is double Olympic gold medallist SEBASTIAN COE.

CLUB CALL
ARSENAL

1. At which ground do they play their home matches?

2. What is their nickname?

3. How many times have they won the First Division Championship?

4. Who was their manager when they first won the League Championship?

5. Against which team did they win the FA Cup at Wembley Stadium in 1930?

6. Who was their regular goalkeeper in their Championship season of 1952-53?

7. In which season did they win the European Fairs Cup by beating Anderlecht in a two-leg final?

8. Which Irish international skippered them when they won the FA Cup in 1979?

9. Who was top scorer in their 1970-71 'double' season?

10. Which former England international holds the record for most League goals for Arsenal in total aggregate?

ANSWERS

SPORTSTANGLE (Page 171): 1 Frank Bruno; 2 Graham Gooch; 3 Steffi Graf; 4 Joe Frazier.

Your Score

Running Total

CLUB CALL
ASTON VILLA

1. At which ground do they play their home matches?

2. What is their nickname?

3. How many times have they won the First Division Championship?

4. Name the England centre-forward who scored a record 49 First Division goals for them in the 1930-31 season?

5. Against which team did they win the FA Cup at Wembley Stadium in 1957?

6. Which Irish international scored two goals for Villa in the 1957 FA Cup Final?

7. Who was manager when they won the First Division Championship in 1980-81?

8. Which England international centre-forward scored their winning goal in the 1982 European Cup Final?

9. From which club did Villa sign Gerry Hitchens in 1957?

10. Who scored their winning goal against Norwich City in the 1975 League Cup Final?

Your Score

Running Total

ANSWERS

THE CHAMPIONS (Page 172): Arsenal, Aston Villa, Burnley, Chelsea, Derby County, Everton, Ipswich Town, Leeds United, Liverpool, Manchester City, Manchester United, Nottingham Forest, Portsmouth, Tottenham, Wolves.

CLUB CALL
BURNLEY

1. At which ground do they play their home matches?

2. What is their nickname?

3. How many times have they won the First Division Championship?

4. Which Burnley defender was voted Footballer of the Year in 1962?

5. Who won 52 caps with Northern Ireland while a regular midfield schemer at Burnley?

6. Against which club were they runners-up in the 1947 FA Cup Final?

7. From which club did they buy Martin Dobson for £300,000 in 1974?

8. Name their famous, dominating chairman during their successful years in the 1960s?

9. Who was their manager when they last won the League Championship?

10. How many times have they won the FA Cup?

ANSWERS

Your Score

Running Total

CLUB CALL
CHELSEA

1. At which ground do they play their home matches?

2. What is their nickname?

3. In which season did they win their only First Division Championship?

4. Which former England centre-forward managed their title-winning team?

5. Against which team did they win the 1970 FA Cup Final?

6. Name the manager who succeeded Tommy Docherty.

7. Who scored their second goal in the 2-1 European Cup Winners' Cup Final win against Real Madrid in 1971?

8. Which England international scored a club record 164 League goals between 1958 and 1970?

9. Name their former skipper who made a club record 655 League appearances.

10. In which year did they sell Ray Wilkins to Manchester United?

Your Score

Running Total

ANSWERS

CLUB CALL
DERBY COUNTY

1. At which ground do they play their home matches?

2. What is their nickname?

3. In which season did they win the First Division Championship for the first time?

4. Who was their manager when they first won the League Championship?

5. Who was their manager when they won the First Division title for the second time?

6. Against which team did they win the FA Cup in 1946?

7. Who scored two goals for Derby in the 1946 FA Cup Final?

8. For which striker did they receive £400,000 from Southampton in 1978?

9. Name their famous player who scored a club record 291 League goals between 1892 and 1906.

10. Who skippered their 1975 League title-winning team?

ANSWERS

CLUB CALL, BURNLEY (Page 175): 1 Turf Moor; 2 The Clarets; 3 Twice; 4 Jimmy Adamson; 5 Jimmy McIlroy; 6 Charlton Athletic; 7 Everton; 8 Bob Lord; 9 Harry Potts; 10 Once (1914).

Your Score

Running Total

CLUB CALL
EVERTON

1. At which ground do they play their home matches?

2. What is their nickname?

3. How many times have they won the First Division Championship?

4. Who was their manager when they won the League Championship in 1969-70?

5. Against which team did they win the FA Cup in 1966?

6. Who scored two goals for Everton in the 1966 FA Cup Final?

7. In which season did they win the European Cup Winners Cup?

8. Who was captain of their 1962-63 League Championship winning team?

9. From which Lancashire club did they sign Alan Ball in 1966?

10. Which manager signed Gary Lineker from Leicester City?

Your Score

Running Total

CLUB CALL
IPSWICH TOWN

1. At which ground do they play their home matches?

2. What is their nickname?

3. In which season did they win their only League Championship?

4. Who was their manager when they won the title?

5. Against which team did they win the FA Cup in 1978?

6. Who was the former England international Bobby Robson succeeded as Ipswich manager?

7. Name the Scottish international who scored a penalty for them in the first leg of the 1981 UEFA Cup Final?

8. Which former England defender played a club record 591 League games for them between 1966 and 1982?

9. Who holds the club record with 203 League goals?

10. Which Northern Ireland international centre-half won 47 caps while with Ipswich?

ANSWERS

CLUB CALL, DERBY COUNTY (Page 177): 1 The Baseball Ground; 2 The Rams; 3 1971-72; 4 Brian Clough; 5 Dave Mackay; 6 Charlton Athletic; 7 Jackie Stamps; 8 Charlie George; 9 Steve Bloomer; 10 Roy McFarland.

Your Score

Running Total

CLUB CALL
LEEDS UNITED

1. At which ground do they play their home matches?

2. How many times have they won the League Championship?

3. Who was their manager when they won the League Championship in 1968-69?

4. Which team did they beat at Wembley in the 1972 FA Cup Final?

5. Who scored the winning goal in the 1972 FA Cup Final?

6. In which season did they win the European Fairs Cup for the first time?

7. Who played a club record 629 League games between 1953 and 1973?

8. Which Scot succeeded Bobby Collins as Leeds skipper?

9. Who was their top scorer in their League title-winning season of 1973-74?

10. Who succeeded Brian Clough as Leeds manager?

Your Score

Running Total

ANSWERS

CLUB CALL
LIVERPOOL

1. At which ground do they play their home matches?

2. What is their nickname?

3. How many times have they won the First Division Championship?

4. Who was their manager when they won the First Division Championship in 1963-64?

5. Which team did they beat 2-1 in the 1965 FA Cup Final?

6. Who scored the winning goal in the 1965 FA Cup Final?

7. In which season did they win the European Cup for the first time?

8. From which club did they buy Kevin Keegan?

9. Who succeeded Bob Paisley as Liverpool manager?

10. Which England international played a club record 640 League games between 1960 and 1978?

ANSWERS

CLUB CALL, IPSWICH TOWN (Page 179): 1 Portman Road; 2 Blues or Town; 3 1961-62; 4 Alf Ramsey; 5 Arsenal; 6 Bill McGarry; 7 John Wark; 8 Mick Mills; 9 Ted Crawford; 10 Allan Hunter.

Your Score

Running Total

CLUB CALL
MANCHESTER CITY

1. At which ground do they play their home matches?

2. How many time have they won the First Division Championship?

3. Who was their manager when they won the League Championship in 1967-68?

4. Which team did they beat 1-0 in the 1969 FA Cup Final?

5. Who scored the winning goal in the 1969 FA Cup Final?

6. Against which team did they win the 1970 European Cup Winners' Cup in a two-leg final?

7. Name the defender who played a club record 565 League games between 1959 and 1976.

8. For which player did they pay Wolves £1,437,500 in 1979?

9. Who succeeded Ron Saunders as manager?

10. Which England midfield schemer was capped 48 times while at Manchester City betweeen 1968 and 1976?

Your Score

Running Total

ANSWERS

CLUB CALL, LEEDS UNITED (Page 180): 1 Elland Road; 2 Twice; 3 Don Revie; 4 Arsenal; 5 Allan Clarke; 6 1967-68; 7 Jack Charlton; 8 Billy Bremner; 9 Mick Jones; 10 Jimmy Adamson.

CLUB CALL
MANCHESTER UNITED

1. At which ground do they play their home matches?

2. What is their nickname?

3. How many times have they won the First Division Championship?

4. Who was their manager when they won the FA Cup in 1948?

5. Name the Scottish international who scored two goals in the 1963 FA Cup Final against Leicester City?

6. In which year did they win the European Cup at Wembley Stadium?

7. Against which team did they win the FA Cup Final in 1977?

8. Who played a club record 606 League games for United between 1956 and 1973?

9. Name the manager who succeeded Frank O'Farrell.

10. Who scored 32 First Division goals in 1959-60?

ANSWERS

CLUB CALL, LIVERPOOL (Page 181): 1 Anfield; 2 Reds or Pool; 3 16 times; 4 Bill Shankly; 5 Leeds United; 6 Ian St John; 7 1976-77; 8 Scunthorpe United; 9 Joe Fagan; 10 Ian Callaghan.

Your Score

Running Total

CLUB CALL
NOTTINGHAM FOREST

1. At which ground do they play their home matches?

2. What is their nickname?

3. In which season did they win the First Division Championship for the only time?

4. Who did Brian Clough succeed as Forest manager?

5. Which team did they beat 1-0 when winning the European Cup for the second time?

6. Who scored the winning goal when they beat Malmo in their first European Cup Final?

7. Name the defender who played a club record 614 League games for Forest between 1951 and 1970?

8. From which club did Forest buy Ian Wallace for £1,250,000 in 1980?

9. Name their goalkeeper in the 1978 League Cup Final.

10. Who was Forest's first post-war manager?

Your
Score

Running
Total

ANSWERS

CLUB CALL, Manchester City (Page 182): 1 Maine Road; 2 Twice; 3 Joe Mercer; 4 Leicester City; 5 Neil Young; 6 Gornik Zabrze; 7 Alan Oakes; 8 Steve Daley; 9 Tony Book; 10 Colin Bell.

CLUB CALL
PORTSMOUTH

1. At which ground do they play their home matches?

2. What is their nickname?

3. How many times have they won the First Division Championship?

4. Who was their manager when they beat Wolves in the FA Cup Final in 1939?

5. In which season did they win the First Division Championship for the first time?

6. Who played a record 764 League games for Portsmouth between 1946 and 1965?

7. From which club did they buy Mark Hateley in 1983?

8. Name the England winger who scored a club record 194 League goals between 1946 and 1960.

9. Who did Alan Ball succeed as Portsmouth manager?

10. Which striker was their top scorer with 22 goals when they won the Third Division title in 1982-83?

Your Score

Running Total

CLUB CALL
TOTTENHAM HOTSPUR

1. At which ground do they play their home matches?

2. What is their nickname?

3. How many times have they won the First Division Championship?

4. Who was their manager when they won the League and Cup double in 1960-61.

5. Against which team did they win the FA Cup at Wembley Stadium in 1961?

6. Who was captain of the 1960-61 double team?

7. Which team did they beat in the 1963 European Cup Winner's Cup Final?

8. Who succeeded Terry Neill as their manager?

9. Which defender played a club record 655 League games between 1969 and 1986?

10. From which club did they buy Clive Allen?

Your Score

Running Total

ANSWERS

CLUB CALL, NOTTINGHAM FOREST (Page 184): 1 City Ground; 2 Reds; 3 1977-78; 4 Allan Brown; 5 SV Hamburg; 6 Trevor Francis; 7 Bob McKinlay; 8 Coventry City; 9 Chris Woods; 10 Billy Walker.

186

CLUB CALL
WOLVES

1. At which ground do they play their home matches?

2. How many times have they won the First Division Championship?

3. Who was manager when they were dominating English football in the 1950s?

4. Name the former England captain who skippered them during their 'golden' years.

5. Which team did they beat 3-1 in the 1949 FA Cup Final?

6. Who was the England winger who scored two goals in their 1960 FA Cup Final win against Blackburn Rovers?

7. Name the full-back who played a club record 501 League games for Wolves between 1967 and 1972?

8. From which club did they buy Andy Gray for £1,175,000 in 1979?

9. Who succeeded Sammy Chung as Wolves manager?

10. Which England goalkeeper played for Wolves in the 1949 FA Cup Final?

ANSWERS

Your Score

Running Total

99

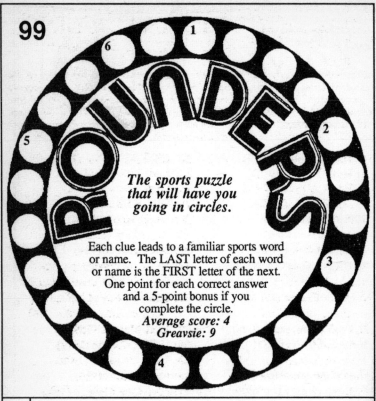

ROUNDERS

The sports puzzle that will have you going in circles.

Each clue leads to a familiar sports word or name. The LAST letter of each word or name is the FIRST letter of the next. One point for each correct answer and a 5-point bonus if you complete the circle.
Average score: 4
Greavsie: 9

1	Surname of the fastest Frenchman on four wheels (5).
2	Do footballers fall into this to control the ball? (4).
3	Surname of Britain's golden girl of the '72 Olympics (6)
4	Jockeys like to be in front on a home one of these (8).
5	Many professional cyclists do it annually in France (4).
6	Johnny, a Dutchman who starred in two World Cups (3).

ANSWERS

Your Score

Running Total

CLUB CALL, TOTTENHAM (Page 186): 1 White Hart Lane; 2 The Lily-whites or Spurs; 3 Twice; 4 Bill Nicholson; 5 Leicester City; 6 Danny Blanchflower; 7 Atletico Madrid; 8 Keith Burkinshaw; 9 Steve Perryman; 10 Queen's Park Rangers.

THE FINAL FLING

Our marathon is nearly over, and here's a final chance to get 100 points on the scoreboard. Listed below are the names of 50 Olympic champions, all of whom won two or more medals. You must name the sport in which they won their titles. Several have been mentioned in earlier puzzles and should give you easy pickings, but others will have you very puzzled! The year after each name is the Games at which they won at least one medal. Two points for each correct answer. Average score: 32. Greavsie: 44

1: Harry Mallin (1924)
2: Ruth Fuchs (1972)
3: Vasili Alexeev (1976)
4: Mark Spitz (1972)
5: Nelli Kim (1976)
6: Al Oerter (1968)
7: Bob Mathias (1952)
8: Daniel Morelon (1972)
9: Laszlo Papp (1956)
10: Dawn Fraser (1964)
11: Abebe Bikila (1960)
12: Teofilo Stevenson ('76)
13: Richard Meade (1972)
14: Pertti Karppinen (1980)
15: Mal Whitfield (1952)
16: Jozef Zapedzki (1972)
17: Toni Sailer (1956)
18: Lars Hall (1956)
19: Vladislav Tretyak ('84)
20: Nikolai Andrianov ('80)
21: Kip Keino (1968)
22: Oliver Kirk (1904)
23: Jean-Claude Killy ('68)
24: John Weissmuller ('28)
25: Lasse Viren (1976)

26: Kornelia Ender (1976)
27: Emil Zatopek (1952)
28: Olga Korbut (1972)
29: Dhyan Chand (1936)
30: Sonja Henie (1936)
31: Ray Ewry (1912)
32: John Kelly (1924)
33: Rosie Mittermaier (1976)
34: Patricia McCormick (1956)
35: Betty Cuthbert (1956)
36: Norbert Schemansky ('64)
37: Paul Masson (1896)
38: Hans Winkler (1972)
39: Irina Rodnina (1980)
40: Nedo Nadi (1920)
41: Charlotte Cooper (1900)
42: Leslie Claudius (1960)
43: Bobby-Joe Morrow (1956)
44: Vitaliy Davidov (1972)
45: Irena Szewinska (1976)
46: Wilhelm Ruska (1972)
47: Vera Caslavska (1968)
48: Paul Radmilovic (1920)
49: Valeri Borzov (1972)
50: Henry Taylor (1908)

ANSWERS   Your Final Total

CLUB CALL, WOLVES (Page 187): 1 Molineux; 2 Three times; 3 Stan Cullis; 4 Billy Wright; 5 Leicester City; 6 Norman Deeley; 7 Derek Parkin; 8 Aston Villa; 9 John Barnwell; 10 Bert Williams.

GREAVSIE'S SPORTS QUIZ CHALLENGE
HOW YOU RATE

> Average score: 1,026 points
> Greavsie's score: 1,431 points
> Maximum score: 2,185 points

2,000 PLUS POINTS

If you have scored more than 2,000 points you are without any question a Sports Mastermind. In fact you should be producing a sports puzzle book of your own! Greavsie bows the knee to you.

1,750 PLUS POINTS

If you have scored between 1,750 and 2,000 points you have an impressive all-round grasp of sport, and you can consider yourself in the top bracket for sports knowledge. Greavsie's looking green!

1,500 PLUS POINTS

If you have scored more than 1,500 points you have given Greavsie a beating and so you win this Challenge match by a comfortable margin. Well done!

ANSWERS

ROUNDERS (Page 188): 1 (Alain) Prost; 2 Trap; 3 (Mary) Peters; 4 Straight; 5 Tour; 6 Rep — ProsTraPeterStraighTouRep.

1,250 PLUS POINTS

If you have scored more than 1,250 points but less than 1,431 you have just failed to beat Greavsie. But congratulations on an excellent challenge.

1,000 PLUS POINTS

If you have scored between 1,000 and 1,250 points, you have given Greavsie a good match but have had to give second best to the Old Groaner. You can claim an average knowledge of sports facts and figures.

750 PLUS POINTS

If you have scored between 750 and 1,000 points that's just below average and you have got to concede defeat to Greavsie. Better luck next time!

LESS THAN 750

If you have scored less than 750 points, Greavsie has given you a thorough beating. Anyway, thanks for playing the game. It proves you are a good sport.

ANSWERS

FINAL FLING (Page 189): 1 Boxing; 2 Athletics (javelin); 3 Weight-lifting; 4 Swimming; 5 Gymnastics; 6 Athletics (discus); 7 Athletics (decathlon); 8 Cycling; 9 Boxing; 10 Swimming; 11 Athletics (marathon); 12 Boxing; 13 Equestrian; 14 Rowing; 15 Athletics (800 metres); 16 Shooting; 17 Skiing; 18 Modern Pentathlon; 19 Ice Hockey; 20 Gymnastics; 21 Athletics; 22 Boxing; 23 Skiing; 24 Swimming; 25 Athletics; 26 Swimming; 27 Athletics; 28 Gymnastics; 29 Hockey; 30 Ice Skating; 31 Athletics (standing jumps); 32 Rowing; 33 Skiing; 34 Diving; 35 Athletics; 36 Weight-lifting; 37 Cycling; 38 Equestrian; 39 Ice Skating; 40 Fencing; 41 Lawn Tennis; 42 Hockey; 43 Athletics; 44 Ice Hockey; 45 Athletics; 46 Judo; 47 Gymnastics; 48 Water Polo; 49 Athletics; 50 Swimming.

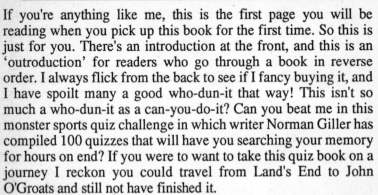

A Funny Old Game
By Jimmy Greaves

If you're anything like me, this is the first page you will be reading when you pick up this book for the first time. So this is just for you. There's an introduction at the front, and this is an 'outroduction' for readers who go through a book in reverse order. I always flick from the back to see if I fancy buying it, and I have spoilt many a good who-dun-it that way! This isn't so much a who-dun-it as a can-you-do-it? Can you beat me in this monster sports quiz challenge in which writer Norman Giller has compiled 100 quizzes that will have you searching your memory for hours on end? If you were to want to take this quiz book on a journey I reckon you could travel from Land's End to John O'Groats and still not have finished it.

You will find a challenge on every page. Your first target will be to beat the average score, then my score. Both my marks and the average score — assessed by testing an across-the-board mix of 100 sports fans of all ages — are printed in the introduction to each quiz. You can keep a check on your score and your running total in the scorecheck boxes at the bottom of each page. The answers to each quiz are at the foot of the next page but one, so you don't have to go searching around here at the back of the book every few minutes to find out whether or not you are right.

Anyway, that's what the book is all about. I hope you now feel sufficiently interested to go to the front and take up Greavsie's Challenge. If you have arrived on this page by the orthodox route, thank you for taking up my challenge. And I'm sure you will now agree that it's a funny old game!

One last thing. Don't forget to pay for the book!

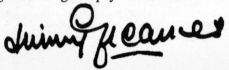